P9-EGL-934

Becoming Facebook

Becoming Facebook

The 10 Challenges That Defined
the Company Disrupting the World

Mike Hoefflinger

AMACOM
American Management Association
New York • Atlanta • Brussels • Chicago • Mexico City • San Francisco
Shanghai • Tokyo • Toronto • Washington, D.C.

Bulk discounts available. For details visit:
www.amacombooks.org/go/specialsales
Or contact special sales:
Phone: 800-250-5308
Email: specialsls@amanet.org
View all the AMACOM titles at: www.amacombooks.org

American Management Association: www.amanet.org
This publication is designed to provide accurate and authoritative information in regard to the subject matter covered. It is sold with the understanding that the publisher is not engaged in rendering legal, accounting, or other professional service. If legal advice or other expert assistance is required, the services of a competent professional person should be sought.

LIBRARY OF CONGRESS CATALOGING-IN-PUBLICATION DATA
Names: Hoefflinger, Mike, author.
Title: Becoming Facebook : the 10 challenges that defined the company that's disrupting the world / Mike Hoefflinger.
Description: New York, NY : AMACOM, [2017] | Includes bibliographical references.
Identifiers: LCCN 2016044188 (print) | LCCN 2017000498 (ebook)
  | ISBN 9780814437964 (hardcover) | ISBN 9780814437971 (eBook)
Subjects: LCSH: Facebook (Firm) | Facebook (Electronic resource)
  | Internet industry—United States. | Online social networks.
Classification: LCC HM743.F33 H64 2017 (print) | LCC HM743.F33 (ebook)
  | DDC
  302.30285—dc23
LC record available at https://lccn.loc.gov/2016044188

10   9   8   7   6   5   4   3   2   1

To makers and builders everywhere.
Everyone risking failure one more time.
And everyone tempted to.

Start today. Don't ever stop.

Contents

Part 3 ■ The Future

Part 4 ■ Parting Thoughts

Preface

In 2009, Mark Zuckerberg was immortalized in Ben Mezrich's *Accidental Billionaires*—a book that starts with the sentence, "It was probably the third cocktail that did the trick" and served as Aaron Sorkin's source material for the movie *The Social Network*—as a morally dubious, socially awkward coder mostly motivated by meeting girls. Facebook, with just 150 million users at the beginning of 2009 and coming off a year with only $270 million in revenue, was considered as uncertain a business as MySpace, which was still the largest social network in the United States.

By the end of 2015, Zuckerberg was feted as one of the greatest CEOs and philanthropists ever, Sheryl Sandberg as not only a model COO but a leading light and voice in equality, and Facebook as a company as respectable—and deserving of credit for changing the world—as Google and Apple. They had grown the number of people who used Facebook by 15 times, become the home to four of the world's top six communication tools (three of which serve more than a billion users monthly), increased their market value by 30 times to over $300 billion and their revenue over 60 times to nearly $18 billion annually.

This book is the story of what happened in those seven years and what may happen in the next ten. From the inside. Facebook's coming-of-age as one of the world's great companies.

As for me, I'm a builder. Have been since 1981 when I got my first Apple][computer. Maybe the only thing I love more than building is to observe great builders. So it's no accident I'm on my second stint in Silicon Valley. The first one was back in 1978 when my dad was on a sabbatical at UC Berkeley and we'd drive around the pre-PC, pre-Internet, pre-iPhone valley and visit Texas Instruments to see their brand-new Speak'n'Spell toy in the lab. The second started in 1990. Twenty-five years later, I'm still here.

I had the good fortune to be at Intel to work on the first microprocessor to have a name and to see the PC take the world by storm in the early 1990s. To work for Andy Grove when the Internet emerged, and we would visit Google's Larry Page and Sergey Brin and their ping-pong table boardroom in Palo Alto, Amazon's Jeff Bezos in a converted hospital building in Seattle, and Loudcloud's Marc Andreessen and Ben Horowitz in an industrial park in Sunnyvale—a decade before they would come to be known simply as venture capital firm a16z. To work for Mark Zuckerberg and Sheryl Sandberg as they built some of the most influential services of the tectonic mobile shift.

As general manager of the Intel Inside program, I had already been a customer of Sandberg's for a year by the time the two of us sat down in a coffee shop in downtown Palo Alto in the fall of 2008 to talk about my joining her team building Facebook's fledgling advertising business. Long story short, Sandberg was very convincing, and seven years later the team had grown Facebook's advertising business by more than 60 times to $18 billion annually, and I had built the global branding, positioning, communication, consulting, and consumer insights teams, for that business who were made up of—as was every team at Facebook—hundreds of the best people in the world in each of their roles looking to make their contribution to Facebook's mission of making the world more open and connected.

It was always intense and never easy, but the story of how Zuckerberg, Sandberg, and Facebook's teams built a business of real consequence—to go along with the largest mobile consumer services in the world—is one of the all-time great Silicon Valley stories. I'm grateful to have been a part of it and thrilled to write it down and share it with you.

I'm not a journalist like Michael Lewis (*Moneyball*) or a professor like Clayton Christensen (*The Innovator's Dilemma*), but I *am* a builder and an observer.

I built with Sheryl and Mark and their 10,000 closest friends.

And these are my observations.

Mike Hoefflinger
Los Altos, California
October 2016

1

Setting the Scene

The Bell Tolls

Figure 1-1. Facebook's closing stock price following its 2012 IPO
(May 18–September 4)

On September 4, 2012, 109 days after standing up in front of an expectant world as the second largest stock market initial public offering (IPO) in US history, Facebook's stock closed at $17.73, 53%—and more than $50 billion in value—below its hopeful origin as not just a public company but as a referendum on social media. (See Figure 1-1.)

1

A referendum on Mark Zuckerberg—the wunderkind who had been fictionally immortalized in an Oscar-winning Aaron Sorkin screenplay— for whom "a million wasn't cool."

A referendum on Zuckerberg's vital business partner, Sheryl Sandberg, and her sparkling record in government and business and passion for equality that had not yet expressed itself in a best-selling book but was on display at TED conferences.

A referendum, it seemed, on the very concept of the new Silicon Valley, which was no longer about either Silicon or its valley as networks of shuttles whisked the young software developers who had inherited this part of the earth to and from their preferred San Francisco playground.

There was no saving grace. No apparent way to talk yourself out of the surrounding facts: the overall economy was recovering, and highly regarded technology companies like Google and Apple—hell, even the NASDAQ—were up 10% in the same time frame.

No. Facebook stood starkly alone in its decline, and $17.73 didn't look like the bottom. BMO Capital was setting their future price estimate at $15, implying Facebook was well on its way to eroding its IPO valuation by a soul-crushing three-quarters. Influential analyst eMarketer announced lower than expected revenue projections for the year. And only a month hence, October 2012 would bring the ending of the post-IPO lockup of 1.2 billion shares of Facebook's stock, introducing a frighteningly large amount of new supply to overwhelm the already flagging demand for the stock.

Facebook's new narrative hued more closely to the dismissed carcasses of once high-flying technology darlings like Groupon, Zynga, and MySpace.

"Facebook was not originally created to be a company," proclaimed its own materials shared with partners to aid them in understanding the company's unique culture. Maybe, the pundits gathering in droves around the declining company suggested, not-a-company is how it would end.

No Moves Left?

One of the biggest reasons the 53% slide felt much worse than merely a halfway point was that at the time only three consumer technology companies had come back from a decline of that scale to thrive and grow beyond their former glory. They are technology royalty: Apple, Google and Amazon. With hall-of-fame CEOs: Steve Jobs, Larry Page, and Jeff Bezos. As of September 4, 2012, however, the vast majority of observers judging Zuckerberg felt—to paraphrase Lloyd Bentsen's infamous debate retort—that he was no Steve Jobs. No Larry Page. No Jeff Bezos.

In public, everyone will gladly caution you not to confuse stock price with intrinsic business value. But behind closed doors, these stock downturns usually brought with them vicious cycles of negative external perception and declining internal morale and productivity. They usually made convenient excuses for new and prospective customers to pull back. Usually made recruiting great talent—especially in the obscenely competitive market that is Silicon Valley—much more difficult. And usually disrupted internal flow while management teams scrambled for answers.

Worse yet, leading up to the IPO, Facebook's leadership—Zuckerberg, Sandberg and others like respected chief financial officer David Ebersmann—had seemingly done everything right. Nine hundred million monthly users. A profitable business. Oversubscribed IPO roadshow. Largest IPO market valuation in the United States.

From the outside, it now appeared, they were out of moves. From the outside, this looked like the end. Or—much worse in the mind of an innovator like Zuckerberg—a long decline to irrelevance similar to the likes of HP and Yahoo. And for 109 days, he had not appeared in public to counter those perceptions.

This is the story of how Facebook got to that point, its amazing recovery and what lies ahead:

- ▸ Chapter 2 shows how everything at Facebook starts with Mark Zuckerberg.

- ▸ Chapters 3–12 are the 10 lessons in Facebook's rise from also-ran to the recovery from the troubled IPO to becoming the reigning juggernaut of the most important shift in consumer media in six decades: the unprecedented rise of mobile screens.

▸ Chapters 13–16 look at the big moves Facebook intends to make in the future and what happens if Facebook wins in all its ambitions.

▸ And Chapters 17–18 dissect how failure is a part of Facebook's success but that even Facebook may eventually get disrupted.

2

Finding Your Inner Zuck

Everything at Facebook starts with Mark Zuckerberg, but it doesn't end there

To tell any Facebook story, you have to first put its lead—Mark Zuckerberg—on stage and give him some context. A path to walk, and a reason to walk it. A tribe to belong to. An origin story from a time before the movie, the hacker's den in Palo Alto and the Harvard dorm room that hints at how this kid from the comfortable embrace of a close, upper-middle-class American family in the leafy Hudson Valley suburb of Dobbs Ferry 20 miles north of New York City would possibly become a global connector whose work may mean more to people in places like Africa, Southeast Asia, Columbia, Egypt and India than it does even to those in the United States.

Steve Jobs, the patron saint of standout CEOs, during his memorable June 2005 Stanford University commencement address, said, "You can't connect the dots looking forward; you can only connect them looking backward."

Looking backward through Zuckerberg's life, we see what Jobs meant: the mission to make the world more open and connected has stayed the same for Zuckerberg since the very beginning, he has simply pursued it at an ever larger scope. A scope so large by now that even he—by his own admission—could not have foreseen it in the beginning.

So we go back to that beginning. To the split-level home on that leafy corner of Russell Place and Northfields Avenue in Dobbs Ferry and a pre-teen Zuckerberg—fresh off having been taught programming basics by his dad—building a simple messaging program dubbed ZuckNet to connect the six Zuckerbergs and the computers in their house with those in his dad's dentist office attached to the house (the Painless Dr. Z they called him in Dobbs Ferry).

Connecting *beyond* Zuckerberg's childhood home is a story of motive and opportunity. Motive because that house was separated from Ardsley High School and his friends by a valley with 10 lanes of traffic in the form of the Saw Mill River Parkway and Interstate 87. And opportunity because Zuckerberg, born in 1984, was an early Millennial growing up in an upper-middle-class suburb, making him a member of the first demographic to have computers and the consumer-accessible Internet throughout their teens, allowing them to feel connected all the time, independent of physical barriers and distances, *and* to build things on top of that connectivity. Zuckerberg has become a global connector not *despite* his somewhat privileged upbringing but precisely because of it.

To be sure, the Saw Mill River Valley is no DMZ, no border fence, no cultural, economic, political or religious barrier, but it nevertheless drove home for Zuckerberg the power and potential of digital connectedness. And, while he—like all of us—would use search engines to navigate *information* on the Internet, he realized in those early days that there was no such tool for *people*. The origins of Zuckerberg as a leader and of Facebook as a company lie in those twin realizations.

But first came CourseMatch, a system that put the social and academic interests of the Harvard community online so students could know more about prospective classmates. Shortly after followed a site with 500 images of Roman art history, shared with the rest of the students in his class to pool notes in order to study for a final exam (on which the students proceeded to get historically high grades). With FaceMash a few months later, he pushed both his development (based on downloading student's pictures after hacking into data on nine of Harvard's 12 houses via local networks or the Internet) and the site's social interactions (asking users to rate the looks of others students) beyond the lines of good taste, copyright law and privacy, landing himself on probation with Harvard and in need of having to apologize to campus women's groups. Without the misstep of FaceMash, however, which taught Zuckerberg not only to respect privacy but to make controlled data sharing a central feature, it is much less likely that he would have launched thefacebook.com at Harvard the way he did in February 2004.

Having conquered Harvard, U.S. universities followed. Then high school students. Then all Americans. Through translations, Facebook expanded to dozens of—and eventually to more than a hundred—countries (more on all this in Chapter 5). Not satisfied with connecting people in just one way, Facebook developed Messenger and acquired Instagram and WhatsApp (more in Chapters 9 and 13). With their fastest growing app ever, Facebook Lite, they began to support all those around the world who can scarcely afford occasional Internet access, and with efforts including satellites, drones the size of 737s and lasers, they are now looking to connect even the unconnected (more in Chapter 14).

Every journey of connecting billions starts with connecting the first six in your own house. Zuckerberg has simply not stopped since. Looking back, it's no exaggeration to say that the 32-year-old has been working to make the world more open and connected for more than two decades.

Member of a Very Small Group

During those two decades, he has become a member of a very small group of people who run consumer technology companies that invent the future for us, create the things we cannot live without, and touch hundreds of millions and sometimes billions of lives. Abstract people that, like Beyoncé or Batman, go by a single name: Grove, Jobs, Bezos, Hastings, Page, Zuckerberg, Musk. They become someone we seemingly cannot know, so we settle for the media—and in very special cases, Aaron Sorkin—possibly explaining them to us in oversimplified shorthand: paranoid, mercurial, focused, renegade, cerebral, socially awkward visionary.

They built the microprocessors in our computers and then had the audacity to make us care about what was "inside." Triggered the advent of the personal computer and ushered in the most sweeping change in consumer technology ever with the iPhone. Built us a store for everything after starting with books out of a garage. Made us "feel lucky" with the quality of search results and launched an operating system now used by 80% of smartphones. Let us watch *what* we wanted *when* we wanted and first beat Blockbuster and then traditional television itself. Wrote down a three-step plan to building the first new public American car company to be founded in a century, proceeded to build the best-selling car in its category—which just happened to be electric—and then received nearly 400,000 preorders for a car that didn't exist. Connected a billion people a day and considered it just a beginning.

They are *very* unique but have three profound similarities (beside the regrettable fact that they are all white men, an important subject for an entire collection of books that still need to be written beyond Sheryl Sandberg's *Lean In*):

1. They have the will to keep acting on an "achievable-unachievable" mission: Because they aim for long-term change at large scale, they are doubted, mocked and eventually competed with. Consistently leading progress toward things that do not yet exist in the face of opposition from the outside—and complexity on the inside—may wear down more ordinary leaders, but not this tribe. Steve Jobs' biggest breakthrough in "building tools for the mind that advance humankind" came thirty years after his first. Jeff Bezos is in his third decade of building "earth's most customer-centric company." Kids born the year Larry Page started "organizing the world's information and making it universally accessible" will be waiting for college acceptance letters this year. Zuckerberg ("make the world more open and connected") and Elon Musk ("accelerate the advent of sustainable transport") are just getting warmed up in the second decades of their missions.

The notion of mission had its defining moment in front of the U.S. Congress on May 25, 1961, when the newly elected John F. Kennedy proposed that "this nation should commit itself to achieving the goal, before this decade is out, of landing a man on the moon and returning him safely to earth." Sadly, the vast majority of corporate versions—the thing we feel compelled to have but dread writing—dramatically undershoot the "stirring (wo)men's souls" bar of Kennedy's moonshot. Only a tiny few have gone on to exceed it. Not satisfied with merely setting a decade-long goal, these "achievable-unachievable" missions are so big they may never be fully realized but allow for victories along the way to sustain the confidence of both their purveyors and consumers. They attract talent and define company culture at all moments, not just the quarterly all-hands and annual shareholders meeting. (You don't have a great mission until people are saying it to each other voluntarily, and you *definitely* don't have a great mission if it still includes the words "revenue," "profit" or "shareholders.")

2. They are "clever-foolish" visionaries: They see things others cannot. Or, better yet, that others dismiss. Foolish ideas are a race to nowhere. Clever ideas that everyone can see are a food fight. The ideas that matter far above all others are clever but *considered* foolish until it's too late for the competition to react.

How hard is it to be clever-foolish? You have to see it before anyone else does, have the confidence to move forward without hesitation amid great uncertainty, build it before anyone else can and then do it all over again if you want to ensure your advantage because even clever ideas that are originally considered foolish eventually reveal themselves. You have to see the opportunity for microprocessors that would go on to make the consumer-scale Internet possible for both PCs and servers two decades before the first web browser. For a consumer-ready computer in 1977, when there was no demand for such a thing. For Internet-based e-commerce in 1994, when consumers thought it was nuts to give out their credit card number on the Internet. For a service named Netflix in 1997 (when we were driving to thousands of Blockbuster stores) that intended to eventually deliver television over the Internet. For a better search engine in 1999 when Yahoo! completely dominated that category. For a social network that connects billions in 2004 when the leaders in the category had a few million users. For a single piece of glass in your pocket connected to everyone everywhere in 2007 when those devices all had physical keyboards and sold a few million high-end units a year. And for an electric car better than everything in its category in 2012 after many decades of abject failure for that very product from the world's biggest carmakers.

3. They foster product-centric Medici Academies that attract the best builders: The success of the kinds of missions they pursue depends on the quality of their products, and that depends on the quality of the people building those products and the means and urgency with which they are building them. These leaders have a very strong point of view about what makes a better future, and they make the time to recruit the best and to work directly with them to create that future.

Five hundred years before Silicon Valley—around 1450—Florentine patriarch Cosimo de Medici began to build facilities, bestow patronage and host Platonic discussion societies for the brightest minds of Renaissance Florence, a practice that continued to flourish as Cosimo's grandson Lorenzo came into power in 1469—at the age of twenty (roughly Zuckerberg's age when he started Facebook)—and ruled until 1492. The Medicis would host and enable the most talented "makers" of their time (including Michelangelo, DaVinci and Botticelli), create supporting resources (such as the Medici Library), set and pursue a vision (humanism, a focus on human agency and science over "revelation") and forward-invest in infrastructure (including architectural commissions).

The reason Silicon Valley's giants are doing the same now is that although people are a company's greatest assets, a more subtle truth is that its very best people are its disproportionately greatest asset. Steve Jobs has said a great maker is 25 times more valuable than an average one. Zuckerberg has said the difference is 100 times. Marc Andreessen thinks five great makers are worth 1,000 average ones. And Bill Gates once said they were 10,000 times more valuable. Even though each of them has acknowledged that their assessments are not scientific, they make it clear how strongly these legendary leaders feel about attracting the best talent.

Jeff Bezos, in his 2016 letter to Amazon shareholders, captured the outsized impact of this effect on business:

> The difference between baseball and business, is that baseball has a truncated outcome distribution. When you swing, no matter how well you connect with the ball, the most runs you can get is four. In business, every once in a while, when you step up to the plate, you can score 1,000 runs. This long-tailed distribution of returns is why it's important to be bold.

It's impossible to be bold without the best people, and for the very best people, it's not a matter of where they *can* work but where they *want* to work. Where can they do what engages them most—keeping in mind that, for these "outlier makers," their efforts are often driven by an emotion deeper than engagement and closer to compulsion—and what has the biggest likelihood of impact on people and the world?

So there it is: "all" you need to be incredibly successful is a clever-foolish visionary with the will to keep acting on his or her achievable-unachievable mission who fosters a product-centric Medici Academy. The members of this group are as valuable as they are rare. As of May 2016, four of the world's six most valuable companies have this kind of leader: Apple (1st), Alphabet (2nd), Facebook (5th), Amazon (6th). And only eight of them have operated in consumer technology in the last forty years: Grove, Jobs, Bezos, Hastings, Page, Zuckerberg, Musk and Uber CEO Travis Kalanick.

That's why you would have given fleeting odds to the kid from Dobbs Ferry joining this group, but join it he has, especially if you can see him in action inside "MPK," the shorthand for Facebook's headquarters in Menlo Park, California.

What Can We Learn from Zuck?

Watching Zuckerberg, however, you're left wondering—as you would be with all *Time* magazine Persons of the Year—how you could possibly emulate him. It would be nearly impossible to learn to do *what* Zuckerberg does: vision and intuition are hard to coach.

We can, however, learn from *how* he does it. Zuckerberg is entirely, consistently, matter-of-factly committed to Facebook's mission. He is out to create change, not to prove himself right or others wrong. To do this—to *really* do this—you have to not only see a great destination, you have to fearlessly and imperviously keep walking toward it. You will look naive and even arrogant to outside observers, and you may be branded delusional—or even "socially dysfunctional" (thanks, Aaron Sorkin)—for appearing not to react to their signals. If you are able to shake off these judgments—and it *will* feel personal at times—you *may* be ready for the hard part, and the key to finding your inner Zuck: **doing is better than dogma**.

Although Zuckerberg is as passionate about his mission as anyone, he is not a preacher but a doer. Both inside Facebook and publicly, he prefers to show rather than tell. Since ZuckNet, with the original development of thefacebook.com, and ever since, he has done the work while others have watched or waited or done both.

To show Facebook employees what the "What would you do if you weren't afraid?" posters around campus mean to him, he took billions of dollars of risk to expand connectivity around the world, acquired Instagram and WhatsApp to protect Facebook's future after spending years building personal relationships with their CEOs, and occasionally failed publicly with products for which he had strongly advocated (here's looking at you, Facebook Home).

Although he is the recognized leader of technology's younger generation, he continues to seek out the leaders that came before him, meeting with Andy Grove about the will to execute, with Jeff Bezos about keeping your eyes on the long term, and with Bill Gates about effective philanthropy with tens of billions of dollars. Even though he structurally controls Facebook's board of directors, he still recruited challenging and highly opinionated thought leaders like entrepreneur, venture capitalist and software-eats-the-world evangelist Marc Andreessen; PayPal mafia kingpin, venture capitalist, futurist and contrarian Peter Thiel; Netflix CEO and old-world television slayer Reed Hastings; and Don Graham, the former owner of *The Washington Post*.

To advance human potential, he doesn't just teach in Menlo Park primary schools. He and his wife (San Francisco pediatrician Priscilla Chan)—who were already among the most prolific *and* youngest philanthropists ever at the time[1]—marked the birth of their first daughter Max in 2015 by pledging 99% of their Facebook holdings (worth $45 billion at the time) to their Chan Zuckerberg Initiative dedicated to driving equality and human potential in the world. It is one of the most profound philanthropic efforts ever announced—as if Bill and Melinda Gates had launched their highly impactful foundation while Gates was still the young CEO of Microsoft—and emblematic of Zuckerberg's learn-faster ethos and inclination to take a risk and determine the best future course sooner rather than later.

To mature into an industry statesperson, he has gone from being the teenager who made regrettable comments about user privacy that emerged in the Winkelvoss trial and showed up at a meeting with venture capitalists in his pajamas to meeting with Chinese President Xi Jinping, speaking at the United Nations on global Internet connectivity and hosting Indian Prime Minister Narendra Modi, all within a few days in September 2015.

To broaden and deepen his perspective on the world in the middle of Facebook's historic rise to global influence, during his 2015 A Year of Books, he read a book every two weeks (including the likes of Vaclav Smil's *Energy: A Beginner's Guide*, Daron Acemoglu and James A. Robinson's *Why Nations Fail*, Michelle Alexander's *The New Jim Crow: Mass Incarceration in the Age of Colorblindness* and Daryl Collins, Jonathan Morduch, Stuart Rutherford and Orlanda Ruthven's *Portfolios of the Poor: How the World's Poor Live on $2 a Day*) and actively discussed them with the nearly 700,000 followers of the project.

To get closer to both his own extended family—Chan's grandparents are Chinese—and the culture and business of the world's most populous market, he spent five years learning Mandarin and then used it in conversations with Chinese politicians and for entire lectures at Tsinghua University in China where he is a member of the Advisory Board of the School of Economics and Management.

To show why he felt the new Facebook Live video product was so valuable, he hosted the likes of President Barack Obama, comedian Jerry Seinfeld and the astronauts of the International Space Station on his own Facebook account—with its 70 million fans—and got more viewers than the vast majority of television shows.

And to face his discomfort with public speaking, he instituted in 2008 a weekly company-wide Q&A—he prefers the hard questions—which to this day remains the heart of Facebook's culture.

Just when we thought Steve Jobs' famous reality distortion field would be the standard by which all future change-makers would be measured, Zuckerberg offers us an approach that may look slightly awkward to the average observer but gives up nothing to Jobs in its effectiveness. Zuckerberg's *doing* does more for getting what he holds dear to jump from him to others at Facebook—and beyond—than any keynote. His Facebook is less a "cult of personality" (he is no Jobs, Oprah Winfrey or Bill Clinton) reliant—and waiting—on a single person than it is a "cult of mission" where employees (down to the intern shipping code for a hundred million users in her first week), partners (entire new media companies like

Vice and Buzzfeed have been built on Facebook's distribution) and users (from Egyptian activists to Vin Diesel and his 100 million fans to Southeast Asian micro businesses reinventing commerce, and from the joy of Chewbacca Mom to the profound fear of Diamond Reynolds) can see Zuckerberg's example and feel not only part of a community but like they can make contributions that may change the world.

2

10 Challenges on the Road from Also-Ran to Juggernaut

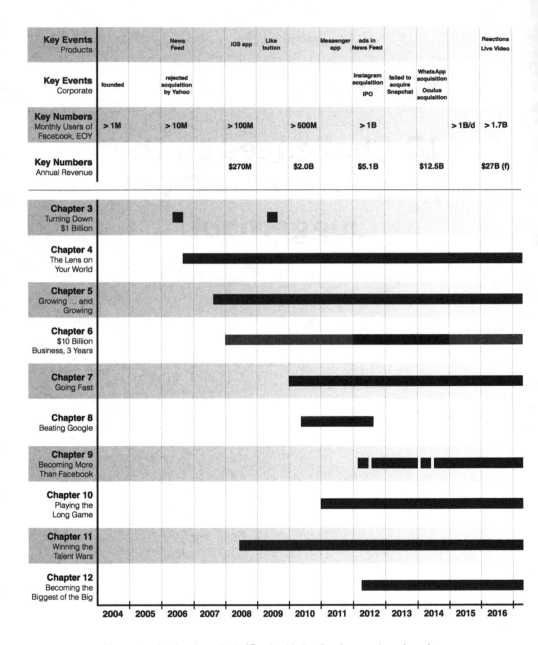

Key Events Products			News Feed		iOS app	Like button		Messenger app	ads in News Feed					Reactions Live Video
Key Events Corporate	founded		rejected acquisition by Yahoo						Instagram acquisition IPO	failed to acquire Snapchat	WhatsApp acquisition Oculus acquisition			
Key Numbers Monthly Users of Facebook, EOY	> 1M		> 10M		> 100M		> 500M		> 1B				> 1B/d	> 1.7B
Key Numbers Annual Revenue					$270M		$2.0B		$5.1B		$12.5B			$27B (f)

Chapter 3 Turning Down $1 Billion														
Chapter 4 The Lens on Your World														
Chapter 5 Growing … and Growing														
Chapter 6 $10 Billion Business, 3 Years														
Chapter 7 Going Fast														
Chapter 8 Beating Google														
Chapter 9 Becoming More Than Facebook														
Chapter 10 Playing the Long Game														
Chapter 11 Winning the Talent Wars														
Chapter 12 Becoming the Biggest of the Big														

| 2004 | 2005 | 2006 | 2007 | 2008 | 2009 | 2010 | 2011 | 2012 | 2013 | 2014 | 2015 | 2016 |

Upcoming chapters in context of Facebook's timeline, key events and numbers

3

How Facebook Turned Down $1 Billion

LESSON 1:
*Know whether this is your next thing
or your last thing.*

Background: Building requires extraordinary willpower to keep executing. Deciding whether to go it on your own or become part of a bigger engine requires knowing the time horizon over which you're likely to have that willpower.

Facebook's Move: Zuckerberg had confidence that he and Facebook could grow all the way to being an independent and thriving public company, so he passed up opportunities to be acquired. Instead, he charted and then pursued—at first in his own mind, then within the company and eventually in front of the world—a 10-year-and-beyond course to make the world more open and connected.

Thought Starter: Are you building a feature, a product, a company or a mission?

In the summer of 2009, Silicon Valley's (and my) past met its (and my) future.

I had worked at Intel from 1992 to 2008 and directly for former CEO Andy Grove from 1999 to 2001. In January 2009, I had moved to working at Facebook after interviewing with its business and engineering leaders as well as with Sandberg and Zuckerberg. When I had reached out to both

Grove and Zuckerberg to see whether they'd be interested in connecting with each other over lunch, both agreed.

We found ourselves sitting at one of the outdoor tables on the small patio behind Facebook's eclectic building adjacent to a Palo Alto neighborhood at the top of South California Avenue. The 50-year-old landmark, affectionately known inside Facebook simply by its street number—1601—and home to the entire company for a brief period prior to the 2011 move into its much larger and ever growing campus in nearby Menlo Park, has since been leveled to make room for larger buildings, dissociating our memories of navigating privacy crises, building client relationships, achieving unprecedented growth and surviving existential competition with Google from the place where we lived them.

Grove was the 72-year-old Silicon Valley legend. Cofounder, CEO and chairman of Intel, the company that more than any other gave the Valley its name and whose microprocessors were responsible for enabling personal computing and cost-effective servers and, with them, the Internet. When Silicon Valley talks about building on the shoulders of giants, it's Grove's shoulders we're talking about. His passing in March 2016 was the end of a world-altering era.

Zuckerberg was the 25-year-old ascendant newcomer building services at a scale and speed only possible because of Grove's legacy.

It was a meeting of the veteran who had made possible a billion connected computers and the rookie on his way to connecting the billion people on those computers.

In the early stages of the conversation, the two circled slowly and respectfully in shallow waters. Grove trying to determine the legitimacy—his bar was notoriously high—of his lunch companion, something I had seen him do in dozens of one-on-one meetings a decade earlier with the likes of Amazon's Jeff Bezos, Yahoo's Jerry Yang, Google's Larry Page and Sergey Brin, eBay's Meg Whitman and LoudCloud's Marc Andreessen and Ben Horowitz (now better known as the venture capital firm a16z). Zuckerberg, in turn, was looking to find common ground with Grove, the statesman who had jumped off the pages of the management bible *Only the Paranoid Survive*—a must-read for self-respecting technology leaders—and who now sat in front of him.

A few minutes in, Grove made his move. A direct question meant not to disrespect or trivialize but to penetrate to a more interesting place for both of them: "How did you turn down Yahoo's $1 billion?"

Yahoo's $1 Billion

Grove's question deserves a quick refresher of the circumstances to which he was referring. Much has been made of the what-could-have-been acquisition offers for Facebook in its early years. Between 2004 and 2007, a string of suitors including Friendster, Google, *The Washington Post*, Viacom, MySpace, News Corp, Viacom again, NBC, Viacom a third time, Yahoo, AOL, Yahoo again, Google again and Microsoft were rumored to have made acquisition overtures of one kind or another to Facebook. The most talked-about was Yahoo's offer in June 2006, said to have initially been worth $1 billion.

Venture capitalist and Facebook board member Peter Thiel, the earliest outside Facebook investor and formerly key player at PayPal, recalled the July 2006 Facebook board meeting between him, fellow venture capitalist Jim Breyer and the then 22-year-old Zuckerberg, held to discuss the 10-figure offer at a time when Facebook was barely two years old and had only eight to nine million users and $20 million in revenue:

> Both Breyer and myself on balance thought we probably should take the money and run. But, Zuckerberg started the meeting like, "This is kind of a formality, just a quick board meeting, it shouldn't take more than 10 minutes. We're obviously not going to sell here." Zuckerberg's argument was that there were all these things we were going to build at Facebook, and he wanted to have a chance to build those products [Facebook was about to open beyond colleges and launch the News Feed]. [Yahoo] had no definite idea about the future. They did not properly value things that did not yet exist. They were, therefore, undervaluing the business.

With a decade of Facebook success behind us, we can recognize Zuckerberg's decision as prescient (judging by 2016 levels, Yahoo undervalued

Facebook by more than 300 times). At the time, however, the young CEO and his board were widely questioned and publicly derided.

Willpower

It was that very derision that had prompted Grove to ask the question: "How did you turn down Yahoo's $1 billion?"

Even in 2009, three years after passing up the acquisition, it was still a defining—and possibly touchy—question since Zuckerberg's decision had not yet been fully vindicated. Facebook's valuation, which had run up to $15 billion in 2008 with Chinese investor Li Ka-Shing's $120 million investment, had declined by as much as 80% to $3.1 billion in the lightly traded private secondary exchange earlier in 2009. Facebook had only just crossed 200 million monthly users globally and was still neck-and-neck with MySpace in the United States. Its eventual $100 billion IPO three years later was not yet a gleam in anyone's eye.

Zuckerberg recognized, however, that Grove was not asking the question in its judgmental form but rather with genuine interest in Zuckerberg's process. He answered it in that spirit.

"I just thought we could do it," he said, referring to growing to a much larger scale and eventually becoming a successful public company with much greater valuation.

While Zuckerberg's answer may seem arrogant on paper—especially in the context of talking to someone who had done what Zuckerberg was still far from accomplishing—Grove saw there was in Zuckerberg no artifice, no arrogance and no lack of understanding of the difficulties that still lay ahead. In that answer, one visionary CEO with willpower recognized another across a chasm of nearly two generations. There was—at that moment—no difference between the two, as the torch passed viscerally from one Silicon Valley era to another. As a footnote to the moment, Zuckerberg would carry that torch forward to being named *Time* magazine's Person of the Year the following year (an honor Grove had received in 1997), and by 2016, Facebook's valuation would go on to eclipse the highest ever reached by Grove's Intel in 2000 (not adjusting for inflation).

Curious, Grove followed up: "Where does that willpower come from?"

Zuckerberg considered the question—possibly for the first time—and concluded simply, "Jewish mother."

Grove, smiling in recognition, eased back in his chair, and the two nodded knowingly in silence. It was a shared moment of huge significance as Grove's own mother had played an outsized role for him throughout his life, especially during his early years growing up in a Jewish family in Hungary where he survived a fascist dictatorship, German military occupation, the Nazi's Final Solution, the siege of Budapest by the Soviet Army and a variety of repressive Communist regimes before fleeing nearly penniless to New York City at the age of 20. Grove captured his mother's profound significance in the dedication of his autobiography *Swimming Across*: "To my mother. Who gave me the gift of life. More than once."

Zuckerberg's upbringing thankfully lacked any of the extreme strife of Grove's, but the two found common ground in the modeling by—and relationship with—their mothers, which had gifted them the endlessly renewable intrinsic asset of willpower (and its siblings resilience, persistence and determination).

Feature, Product, Company or Mission?

As we pull back from Grove, Zuckerberg and the patio behind 1601, it becomes clear that as much as (in Peter Thiel's words) "the most successful businesses have an idea for the future that's very different from the present," a gutsy vision is not enough. You have to know over what time frame you can sustain the willpower necessary to maintain the trajectory to accomplish that vision.

It takes less than a year to build a *feature* (like FriendFeed or Cover-Flow), and you can create tens of millions of dollars of value doing so. In a little more than a year or two, you can create a *product* (like Siri, Android or Instagram), and we've seen that valued as high as a billion dollars. To build a *company* (like LinkedIn or SAP) takes many years and can create tens of billions of dollars of value. Pursuing a *mission*, however, is a matter of decades (Tesla is in its second, as is Facebook; Google is a few years from its third; Amazon is in its third and Apple in its fifth) on the road to possibly creating hundreds of billions of dollars of value. (See Table 3.1.)

	Time	Possible Value
Feature	Months	$n0,000,000
Product	Year	$n00,000,000
Company	Years	$n0,000,000,000
Mission	Decades	$n00,000,000,000

Table 3-1. Time frame and possible value of various business objectives

The higher your aiming point, however, the greater are both the necessary trajectory and the time over which it has to be sustained. Every extra day is another opportunity for fatigue to sneak in. A good-enough-isn't mistake here, a hope-is-not-a-strategy moment of weakness there. And the longer you last, the more likely you are to become a victim of your success and the dreaded if-you-always-do-what-you've-always-done-you'll-always-get-what-you've-always-gotten outcome.

The question of whether to build a feature, product, company or mission has no "right" answer. Innovation comes in all sizes and time frames, and success has as many definitions. What you *do* need, however, are honesty and clarity in assessing to which of these goals you and your idea(s) are best suited. You cannot build a mission in a few years, and you cannot take many years to build a product.

Zuckerberg's horizon is clear. During that July 2006 Facebook board meeting, Thiel and Breyer—his most respected advisors leaning in the direction of ending Facebook's road at being a mere product—reminded Zuckerberg that he stood to personally make $250 million if he accepted Yahoo's acquisition bid. Zuckerberg said that he would only use the money to start another social network and that he liked the one he had. By 2006, Zuckerberg had clearly set his sights on a decades-long mission to make the world more open and connected, and he has shown in the ten years since—to borrow from both the title and intention of Grove's autobiography—that he has the stamina to "swim across."

What is *your* horizon?

4

How Facebook Became Your Lens on the World

LESSON 2:
Add by subtracting.

Background: With a screen in everyone's pocket connected to everyone and everything everywhere all the time, your customers' biggest need is not for more things but for fewer things that matter more.

Facebook's Move: Facebook introduced the News Feed—and its all-important algorithm selecting content from the people and things you care about—and has been vigilant in the decade since to constantly increase the perceived quality of News Feed even as Facebook grew in size by 100 times.

Thought Starter: What part of the world are you making easier for your customers to digest?

More than any other single person, Chris Cox is responsible for your lens on the world.

If Mark Zuckerberg is Facebook's brain and Chief Operating Officer Sheryl Sandberg its heart, then Cox—chief product officer—is its soul, as empathetic to 2G cell phone users in developing countries (Cox's wife, filmmaker Visra Vichit-Vadakan, is the granddaughter of a Thai politician, historian and novelist) as he is to his early-adopter friends in San Francisco and his English teacher mom back in Winnetka, Illinois.

He is so critical to Facebook's people and products that more than a decade into his time with the company, he still leads the most important part of Facebook's weekly on-boarding of new employees: the story of Facebook's mission to make the world more open and connected. He has given this talk to employees and customers literally hundreds of times. I've heard him give it at least a dozen. It's as engaging and relevant today as it has ever been because he cannot contain his enthusiasm for what technology can make possible for people. For how the work of Facebook and others is a natural expansion of the pace and scale of media that goes back to the Gutenberg press and language itself and the future of which was imagined by Cox's favorite visionary, Marshall McLuhan, who famously foresaw a version of the Internet and World Wide Web 30 years before it came to be.

Listening to Cox's narrative, it dawns on the room that what is possible today with smartphones and technologies like Facebook and others was considered science fiction a mere 20 years ago. His interest in connecting people runs so deep that by the end of the session, Facebook's mission—which in the wrong hands could come across as corny and overreaching—feels like precisely the thing you would want to be a part of.

Cox himself connected to that mission back in 2005. At the urging of then roommate and early Facebook employee Ezra Callahan, Cox—at the time a graduate student working on artificial intelligence and natural language processing at nearby Stanford University—arrived unceremoniously on his bike at the very unceremonious Palo Alto offices of Facebook. This upstart would most likely not be right for him. A few conversations later, however, having listened to some of Zuckerberg's cofounders describe the opportunity to connect people far beyond the college website that was publicly evident at the time, Cox wound up calling his mom to tell her he'd be joining Facebook as a software engineer. A year later, he and the team would build and launch Facebook's most important feature: News Feed.

His impact on Facebook was perhaps best captured by Lori Goler—Facebook's People vice president since Cox's return to the product side of the business in 2008—on the 10th anniversary of his start at Facebook: "Facebook is what it is—inside and out—because of you."

News Feed, or the Unexpected Virtue of a Deeply Unpopular Launch

As popular as Cox is, his first big product launch very much was not. Heading into 2006, Facebook was big with its college audience and had six million users, but the product team was observing—the staggering amounts of data Facebook's users generate hold many crucial lessons—that people were liberally clicking through other people's profiles but lacked a central, easy way of answering their biggest question: "What's going on?"

It was a missed opportunity to essentially become the search engine of your life.

In that realization—that connections matter only to the extent that interesting information flows easily between them—was borne the idea for News Feed, a continually updated, roughly reverse chronological listing in the middle of your Facebook page of the most important goings-on among the people and things to which you were connected that included status updates, wall posts, photos and people tagged in photos, events, group activities and new connections. It was a complex technical undertaking, exceeding even what was required by the likes of Google's search technologies. Constantly observing activity across your connections and determining which of the more than 1,500 daily updates available to the average user would be distilled down to the approximately 300 items that would be shown in order to increase the feeling of relevance and decrease the feeling of being overwhelmed required complex calculations using hundreds of pieces of data unique to you and to your engagement with Facebook generally and your connections specifically. It turns out, however, that wouldn't be the hardest part.

Facebook News Feed launched on September 5, 2006. It did not go well. After the announcement of the feature early that Tuesday morning by Facebook's first female engineer, Ruchi Sanghvi, a somewhat unexpected consequence quickly reared its head: News Feed had accomplished its purpose of making it easier to see what was going on across your connections, but in the process it had pushed the third rail issue of your privacy settings—which control who across the social network would see what about you—into the limelight.

While News Feed respected your existing privacy settings, seeing that photo you were tagged in, the relationship status update or group comment front and center on your home page instead of the relative backwaters of your profile page could be unsettling to some.

By the end of the day, Facebook groups—some numbering in the hundreds of thousands and seemingly oblivious to the irony of their rapid rise to prominence owing to the promotion in the very News Feed they were opposing—had formed against the change. Facebook boycotts were being suggested.

By 10 p.m., Zuckerberg himself had to respond. His note, titled "Calm down. Breathe. We hear you," is a microcosm of his approach to Facebook and its community. He acknowledged how the community is responding, restated News Feed's purpose and the commitment to privacy settings—the slings and arrows of which Facebook continually endures as both its pioneer and largest purveyor—and continued, undaunted, toward the future. He knows that without an engaged community being served by the product, there is no connected future but does not sacrifice his belief in how best to move toward that future.

Later that week, Facebook released more granular privacy controls to both remind people of and give them more control over how content makes its way to their and other people's News Feeds.

It was, however, implicitly clear that News Feed was here to stay.

Nearly a decade later, delivering over 200 million stories to screens worldwide *every minute*, Facebook's News Feed has become one of the greatest media ever. Its "personal newspaper"—mine is very different from yours—is the crucial yin to the yang of Facebook's focus on authentic identity across its users. Merely being connected to real people and things you know and care about (e.g., Friendster), or just having a constant stream of unfiltered news from sources you know less personally (e.g., Twitter), would not be as powerful.

Taken together, the combination of authentic identity and News Feed are responsible for Facebook's unrivaled degree of engagement and size.

Once Every Waking Hour

You might have rolled your eyes at the suggestion that Facebook's News Feed is one of the greatest media ever. Could it really be as important as television? The telephone? Newspapers? Music? E-mail? Google?

It could be, and in some ways it already is.

A medium is a means through which we sense (and possibly affect) one another and the world. With time spent on digital media starting to exceed time spent on any other medium—including television (and half of all adults and 70% of 18- to 34-year-olds use Facebook *while* watching TV[1])—back in 2013, it's useful to take a closer look at how we sense and affect the world in digital. With you on one side and the world on the other, there are four media in between, as shown in Figure 4-1.

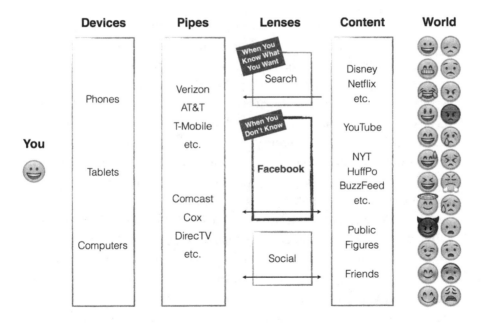

Figure 4-1. The flow of information between you and the world

Closest to you are **devices,** such as your phone, tablet or computer, and **pipes,** such as your cellular provider or cable company. Closest to the world are **content** sources that engage in understanding and interpreting the world from organizations like *The New York Times*, Buzzfeed or Vice and Disney, Netflix or YouTube to public figures like Mark Cuban, Kim Kardashian or Barack Obama to a collection of particularly important people: your friends.

The layers of devices and channels closest to you are more or less replaceable with one another. Whether you have an Android phone or an iPhone or a computer and are on the Internet via Verizon or Comcast, the world isn't appreciably different. The layer of content closest to the world has some big players, but none big enough to amount to significant global influence by themselves any longer (*The New York Times* is a paragon of journalism but is just one of hundreds of different observations of the world in your life).

The layer that makes the biggest difference to you nowadays actually consists of the **lenses** that help you make sense of the onslaught of information that the digital world has brought us. Seventy years ago, newspapers were your all-in-one device (paper), pipe (paperboy), lens (editor) *and* content (stories). Fifty years ago, the three national television networks offered a combined pipe (over-the-air broadcasts), lens (Walter Cronkite) and content (reporters), which you received at your device (television set). A quarter century ago, the arrival of two-way pipes (Internet) and interactive devices (PCs) made dedicated lenses both possible and necessary (Yahoo!'s directory and subsequent search engine) and in doing so downgraded millions of sources to "mere" content. Nothing in media, however, would rival the rise over the last decade of high-speed, wireless two-way pipes and devices (smartphones), which completed the ascension of lenses into a dominant position, particularly two classes of lenses and the dominant provider in each: (1) what you do when you know what you want (search, dominated globally by Google), and (2) what you do when you *don't* know what you want (the implicit "What's going on?" of social media, dominated globally by Facebook in the form of News Feed).

As much as you still have direct relationships with content—the likes of Netflix or your friends—lenses have a disproportionately large influence on how you sense the world, and it turns out that the two primary lenses are not equally important:

> We access search on average three to five times a day, but Facebook on average 10 to 15 times a day. We *don't* know what we want three times as often as we *do* know. We don't know what we want roughly *once every waking hour*.

As a more specific example of the dominance of Facebook's lens, take entertainment-related content: Facebook is the source of new information, information that people wouldn't be aware of otherwise and information relevant to their interests for two to nearly three times as many people as the next closest digital source.

To see just how powerful the News Feed lens is for people *and* Facebook, consider this:

▸ **Facebook has summarily replaced portals**: While Facebook has over 1 billion daily users (with 90% visiting via mobile), Yahoo's home page—the former champion of lenses—has only 53 million[2] (just 20% of which visit on mobile).

▸ **The lens the Internet depends on the most is Facebook's**: According to parse.ly, in January and February of 2016, Facebook's News Feed accounted for 41% of traffic referrals to the hundreds of news sites tracked by the service (all of Google accounted for 39% and the next closest source—Yahoo!—for a mere 4%). Even other giants depend most on Facebook: it generates more traffic to YouTube, which has 1 billion monthly users, than any other source, including all Google (YouTube's parent company) sources combined.

▸ **Facebook plays an outsized role in how we consider new products**: In a 2015 study, Facebook's consumer insights team discovered that in the 24-day consideration period of subjects in the market for a new phone, they visited Facebook 201 times, search 23 times and the websites of the companies making the phones a mere two times.

Aside from its engaging, endless nature, News Feed has benefited from two giant forces during its decade of ascendency.

1. The shift to mobile: People's shift to mobile as their favorite devices around the world—launched in earnest with the iPhone—has been nothing short of a revolution. Cisco now predicts that by 2020 there will be more people with mobile phones (5.4 billion) than electricity (5.3 billion) and running water (3.5 billion) and nearly twice as many as have cars (2.8 billion).

Riding, enabling or—best case—encouraging this trend is paramount to any player in the digital ecosystem, but most especially the lenses.

In ways even Zuckerberg and Cox could scarcely have foreseen in 2006, the endless vertical scrolling column of bite-sized visual stories in News Feed is utterly perfect for the handheld, thumb-controlled vertical form factor of our phones and the frequent short engagements we have with them. The forced focus on a single column in your hand, combined with the visceral feeling of flow provided by a touch-based interface, make for a near perfect physical manifestation of the abstract goal of News Feed to show information across your connections.

Looking backward from the comfort of 2016, it is clear that we went through an interface transition from using windows for desktop computing to using feeds for mobile that was rung in with Steve Jobs' demonstration of touch-based inertial scrolling at the January 2007 launch of the iPhone.

Unlike typical desktop designs like portals with multiple columns and longer-form content, which found themselves struggling to transition to phones, News Feed became even more engaging as Facebook first built a mobile website in 2007 and then launched a mobile app—created by Facebook engineer Joe Hewitt—the day Apple launched its App Store in July 2008. According to analytics firm App Annie, as of September 2015 the Facebook app continued to rein globally as the most downloaded iPhone app ever.

However, it's not just that the shift to mobile was a benefit to News Feed. To put a finer point on things, News Feed would have failed had it not been so well suited to mobile.

2. Scale as Benefit: The second force is an inversion of the typical challenges of content businesses. Growth is a burden for content businesses, impacting both quality and efficiency. Whether they are a news organization or an entertainment company, they have to generate more content at the same levels of quality we were used to when they were smaller and spend increasingly to do so, each additional effort carrying incremental risk of not hitting the bull's-eye of our tastes as well as the one before it. Eventually, it becomes difficult to stay on top in the "hits business."

A lens like Facebook News Feed gets better *and* more efficient as more people use it because more content from more people becomes available—for free—to choose from for the relatively constant number of stories that are served to you every day, and the fixed costs such as data centers, which play a much bigger role in technology businesses than per-user marginal costs, are amortized over more people generating more advertising revenue.

Lenses are two-sided marketplaces matching people with content. The marketplace gets paid to make the match while not incurring any costs for making the content or the roads that lead to the marketplace. While Google benefits from a similar two-sided dynamic and has the same people on one side of its marketplace as Facebook, Facebook has more content being generated on the other side of its marketplace as well as people coming to its marketplace more often.

News Feed's rise to becoming the lens to your world—although not without its hiccups—has been meteoric. While many at Facebook have worked on it over the years—including long-time Facebook product managers and culture-keepers like Peter Deng, Will Cathcart and Adam Mosseri, Cox has been its constant and nurturing parent since birth.

Keeping Your Lens Clean, Well Lit, and Interesting

News Feed's impact on the world is real and important. Yes, it tries to show you the viral video you're likely to enjoy the most, but it bears much greater responsibilities. Responsibility for what it shows you. What it fails to show you. Whether it allows itself to be taken advantage of by spammers and click-baiters. Which kings it is making (hello, Buzzfeed). Which kings it is dethroning (goodbye, Zynga). Which causes it has helped, up to and including revolutions involving entire peoples and countries. And which it failed to give enough of a stage. Which moment of cyber-bullying it prevented through its peer-reporting tools and which it is not yet capable of interdicting. Facebook understands the gravity of this and has made News Feed's goal and values explicit to explain the "why" of News Feed, not just the "what," at http://newsfeed.fb.com ("Show you the stories that matter most to you," "Friends and family come first," "Your feed should inform," "Your feed should entertain," "A platform for all ideas," "Authentic communication," "You control the experience" and "Constant iteration").

News Feed—and Cox as its parent—are responsible to you. And, as the thing making Facebook more engaging than any other service, the two are nearly entirely responsible for the well-being of the company. Facebook's business and its ability to build the future Zuckerberg envisions is increasingly counting on Facebook's many other products and efforts to be supported by News Feed in the way Google's "moonshots" are made possible by its search business.

To live up to that lofty responsibility, News Feed's algorithm, as well as its interface and abilities, is constantly evolving.

After beginning its life by merely understanding clicks, comments, shares, hiding and reported spam back in 2006, News Feed received a massive lift in capability with the arrival of the Like button in February 2009, which created nearly ten times as much engagement data—the News Feed algorithm's oxygen—as mere comments had before it and was used roughly a trillion times (yes, a thousand billion times) in the first three years of its existence.

Over the years, understanding people's behavior beyond simply engaging with a story got increasingly sophisticated, as Facebook took into consideration how long you dwelled on a story in your News Feed relative to the average amount of time you spend with all stories. It also began to account for clicks that didn't signal relevance, such as click-bait headlines that got you to click on an article but whose contents failed to engage you, causing you to return quickly to Facebook, known as a "bounce." Second-order effects like how quickly Likes on an item started to accumulate, whether links shared by your friends were also trending more broadly on Facebook and behavior around videos—at 8 billion views a day as of 2015, a crucial piece of News Feed—such as turning on sound, high-definition or full-screen options started to play a role in how quickly, as well as how high in your News Feed, items were shown.

Beyond just silently observing users, Facebook also started to engage people directly in assessing the quality of their News Feed with surveys of hundreds of thousands of users about which items in their News Feed they would actually prefer to see, as well as explicit features that allow you to unfollow certain people and things to avoid seeing items from them in News Feed and to specify whether you would like to see items from certain people or things first, or less.

To deal with both your reaction to a story and also the origin of that story when it comes from a Page—rather than a friend—you have connected with, Facebook has constructed sophisticated insights tools, provided best practices and even implemented rules around overly promotional content and the amount of text in images in order to reduce the amount of low-quality content that would run afoul of people's expectations entering the system from publishers and businesses.

As an example of the subtlety of Facebook's approach to the algorithm, consider their June 2016 announcement that content from friends and family would be given higher priority than content from the Pages of publishers and businesses. Consistent with News Feed's value that "friends and family come first," this introduced a significant increase in priority that a link from, say, *The New York Times* that your friend had shared would receive relative to *The New York Times* itself sharing that link. As obvious as this change appears on the surface—I would consider a link to the story shared by my friend more than the original story even if I am connected to *The New York Times* on Facebook—it carries with it a potentially negative impact on the unpaid distribution that publishers and businesses receive for their posts, possibly diminishing Facebook's value to these participants and therefore their emphasis on operating on the platform and their business relationship with Facebook. Facebook has to continually trust that what is good for people will always be best for the platform and for all the participants on it.

But all of that is not enough for the most important lens on your world because sometimes you Like a baby photo because you feel socially obligated, not because you actually like it and don't want to (and therefore shouldn't) be shown more baby photos. So, in 2014 Facebook started to engage Facebook users in its 'Feed Quality Panel,' beginning with a pilot program of several hundred people in an office building in Knoxville, Tennessee, who work as contractors to provide extensive daily quantitative and qualitative reports on what they saw in their feed and—more importantly—what they actually *wanted* to see in their feed by rating dozens of their own News Feed stories on a scale from 1 to 5 and reordering the feed they saw the way they would have wanted to see it. The panel is so valuable that it has since been expanded around the world.

As all these new signals are turned into refinements of the algorithm, the changes are rolled out exceedingly carefully to Facebook's gigantic user base.

It starts with an offline simulation, then testing among Facebook's thousands of employees, followed by a small fraction—commonly 1%—of Facebook's users, and finally a complete rollout, although even then a so-called holdout group is retained on the prior version of the algorithm to continue assessing impact. And 24×7, the News Feed team observes data from the News Feed, including engagement and time spent, and has alarms to detect any disturbances.

In addition to evolving how things are chosen for you in News Feed, the team is constantly looking to improve both what those things can be—from status updates to photos to videos to 360-degree videos and even the ability for people to broadcast live video, which was fast becoming another big draw for the kind of public and celebrity figures Facebook wants to keep active on its platform rather than lose to emergent ones like Twitter-owned Periscope or Snapchat and which could even lead to you watching TV, including the NFL, in your News Feed—as well as how you can engage with them.

The year 2016 marked an important time for both *what* you saw, and *how* you engaged with it as the company launched Instant Articles and Reactions.

Instant Articles are a way to bring richer, more interactive content from other web pages directly into your Facebook News Feed—and at much greater speed than mobile users are accustomed to due to the content being cached by Facebook ahead of people engaging with it—that had first been introduced in the well received but ultimately unsuccessful

Paper app the company had launched in 2014. Beyond simply bringing more richness to News Feed, there is also a very real possibility that Instant Articles tighten Facebook's stranglehold on "being the Internet"— or at least being perceived to be—as they bring more content into the Facebook environment considered less open than the Internet at large. To counter, Google has launched its own Accelerated Mobile Pages program, which features web pages using Google's alternative to Instant Articles more prominently in Google's search results, a benefit as appealing as appearing more quickly and richly in Facebook's News Feed.

Expect to continue to see an endless arms race between Facebook and Google over how best to serve you when you *know* what you want (search/ Google) and when you *don't* (discovery/Facebook), including the long-term pursuit of ads that don't *feel* like ads.

Facebook also introduced Reactions in News Feed, the first refinement of the Like button since its launch, which had been carefully considered by Cox and the team for years to allow for more expressive responses to stories (Like, Love, HaHa, Wow, Sad and Angry), while preventing the overly negative discourse the company had feared from the much discussed Dislike button. Beyond creating a feeling of more diverse expression when responding to something you see on Facebook, Reactions also have the long-term potential to refine Facebook's understanding of what particular content—and people—mean to you and create an even more fitting selection of content for you in News Feed. Diversifying a signal Facebook gets from people billions of times per day also creates a new opportunity for better mutual understanding between people and advertisers whose ads will also have the new range of Reactions.

As with all changes, you can be sure Facebook will be careful and attentive to keeping your lens clean.

The Long Future of News Feed . . . and Chris Cox

By virtue of Zuckerberg and Cox's focus and the team's measurement, News Feed will only become a more engaging lens in terms of both time spent and actions taken. However, in the long-view world of Zuckerberg, instead of simply letting this big winner ride, they are already hedging for the future, even allowing for a distant time in which Facebook itself may not dominate but the mission of Facebook Inc. continues undaunted.

Whether it is feeds with different algorithms (e.g., Facebook-owned Instagram), new types of feeds like messaging products (e.g., Facebook-owned WhatsApp, Messenger and human-assisted artificial intelligence service M), new interfaces for future screens with no edges (e.g., Facebook-owned Virtual Reality headset maker Oculus) or even telepathic messaging in the distant, scoff-at-your-own-risk future, Zuckerberg and Cox have their bases covered when it comes to being the lenses on your world (more on all that in Chapters 9, 13 and 15).

And as has been the case since 2006, you can count on every Facebook product having in its design a little bit of what Chris Cox is like in person: step back so that other people can step forward.

5

How Facebook Grows . . . and Grows

Ben Mezrich's *Accidental Billionaires* painted the early days of Facebook as a story of looking for one thing—acceptance in Harvard's rarefied Final Clubs—and bungling into another—an ascendant global social network.

Even as the book was coming out in 2009, however, behind the closed doors in Palo Alto, Facebook was anything but accidental. They were deep into becoming one of the best deliberate growth engines of all time. Facebook's success was not manifest destiny. Not "build it and they will come." It was, from the beginning, a conscious pursuit of constant growth. (See Figure 5-1.)

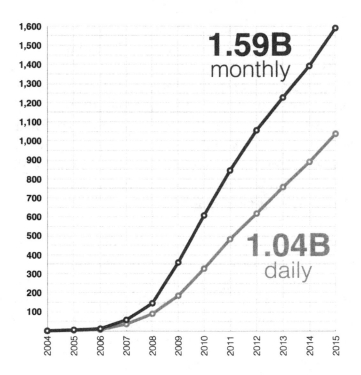

Figure 5-1. Growth of Facebook's monthly and daily active users globally (millions)[1]

And that pursuit wouldn't get difficult at 1.5 billion people, or 1 billion, or even 500 million. It would get difficult much, much earlier than that.

Hitting a Wall

Everything began, of course, at Harvard on February 4, 2004. Using the three-decade-old medium of e-mail to bootstrap their brand-new medium, Facebook's founders invited friends and sent messages to campus mailing lists—the predominant way to form digital groups at that time—to join their new creation, The Facebook, to connect with their friends, to see who else was in their classes and to stay in touch. After new users had signed up for Facebook, they would then be encouraged to invite their friends. In the first week, about half of Harvard's undergrads had registered.

Opening to Harvard was followed carefully by opening to Columbia, Stanford and Yale later that February. The three were chosen not only to carefully manage the process of increasing the size of Facebook without breaking the team's nascent infrastructure but also because the three campuses had some of the most established local social networks at the time. If they could win there, the fledgling crew really might be onto something.

Cornell, Dartmouth, University of Pennsylvania, MIT, Boston University and New York University followed in March, and then Brown, Princeton, UC Berkeley, Duke, Georgetown, University of Virginia, Boston College, Tufts, Northeastern, University of Illinois, University of Florida, Wellesley, University of Michigan, Michigan State, Northwestern, UCLA, Emory, University of North Carolina, Tulane and University of Chicago came on board in April.

At that time, cross-school friend connections were implemented—someone from school A could invite someone from school B—which were a major factor in disrupting any established but highly local social networks. We'll see the importance of this "exogenous" mechanic repeat itself at a much larger scale a little later in the story.

Three months after launch, Facebook had a total of 30 schools and 100,000 members.

The rest of U.S. college campuses followed throughout 2004, and the year ended with Facebook having a million users.

In September 2005, Facebook opened to U.S. high schools and to 20 universities in the UK, and by the end of 2005, it was available at 2,000 colleges and 25,000 high schools in the United States, as well as universities in Canada, Mexico, the UK, Australia, New Zealand and Ireland.

By September 2006, Facebook had grown to about 10 million users and had made the momentous decision that could have ended it all—my *mom* is on Facebook?—to open Facebook to everyone.

With a great sigh of relief, a year later Facebook had grown to 50 million users.

And then they hit a wall.

Getting the Band Together

With growth stalled in late 2007, some very large questions faced Zuckerberg and the team. Why are we stalling? Why had even MySpace (remember, in 2007, Facebook was not yet the leader) been stalled around 100 million users for the better part of six months?

Was there a chance social networking just isn't interesting to more than 100 million people?

There were enough questions that everyone agreed a team had to be put in place to redouble the deliberateness of Facebook's growth.

The team's leader would be brash Sri Lankan–born, Canadian-raised, recovering investment banker, product manager, venture capitalist and self-declared merchant of progress Chamath Palihapitiya. The 31-year-old had just joined Facebook with relevant experience working on small teams for products with large user bases, including music application WinAmp and AOL instant messaging products AIM and ICQ. Palihapitiya's leadership style blends an often-wrong-but-never-in-doubt confidence that hovers just this side of arrogance with an intense do-the-work pragmatism that proved just the right cocktail for Facebook at the time. His team would look-try-measure-repeat their way to success, and Palihapitiya had direct lines to Zuckerberg and Facebook's engineering, infrastructure and product leadership to get the necessary help.

The team's international conscience came from Spanish surfer and recently minted Stanford MBA Javier Olivan. Brought in by Palihapitiya in late 2007, the 30-year-old Olivan had founded a small social network in Spain and came with an engineering and product management background from the European wireless telephone industry, which was growing faster than the American mobile industry at the time and gave him important background for the mobile wave ahead.

Their analytical mind would be the intense, Cambridge-educated Internet marketing savant Alex Schultz. Arriving at Facebook in November 2007, Schultz at age 25 already had 10 years of experience in Internet marketing, having gotten his start with search engine optimization in the pre-Google days for his personal website paperairplanes.co.uk, which he maintains to this day as his personal workbench for the kinds of marketing that he and his team do at a global scale for Facebook. After Internet marketing stints for eBay in the UK and United States, Schultz had the disciplined foundation of picking a target and optimizing for it, from which an even more sophisticated growth engine could evolve. It didn't hurt that he combined passion and urgency in a way perhaps best summed up by one his favorite quotes—from General George S. Patton no less:

> A good plan, violently executed now is better than a perfect plan next week.

Finally, the team's product and people sensibility—a perfect yin to Schultz's analytical yang—would be provided by the quiet, almost elfin, Naomi Gleit. At 22, Gleit had been so convinced of Facebook's eventual success before they even had a million users that in her final year in Stanford's Science Technology and Society program she wrote a paper on how Facebook had beaten local social network Club Nexus and then proceeded to hound Facebook for a job until she got one, starting in 2005 in one of the first nonengineering roles at the company. Having volunteered in Botswana, taught on a Navajo reservation and lived in a Buddhist monastery in Thailand, she was deeply connected to her team's mission to "remove barriers and make Facebook available to everyone in the world."

With Palihapitiya, Olivan, Schultz and Gleit at the core, the team—which would grow to well over 100 people over the years—would go about attacking the wall.

The Math of Growth

Attacking walls is not glamorous work. Not work that is often visible. Not work that even works much of the time. Schultz describes the daily, never ending effort this way:

> If you can run more experiments than the next guy, if you can be hungry for growth, if you can fight and die for every extra user and you stay up late at night to get those extra users, to run those experiments, to get the data, and do it over and over and over again, you will grow faster.

But before we crack open the doors on the specifics of what the team has done over the years, what *is* growth?

You don't need to know calculus to understand the math of growth. It is as simple as it is unforgiving. For a service like Facebook, the number of active users in any particular period t—a month, for example—is the following:

$$\text{Active}_t = \text{New}_t + \text{Retained}_{t-1} + \text{Resurrected}_{t-[n]} - \text{Churned}_{t-1}$$

Although your users make up one large group, they are composed of four very different cohorts:

▸ **New**: People who joined for the first time in the current period via acquisition and activation techniques. They have the least experience with the product and need to be nurtured carefully.

▸ **Retained**: People who used the product in the current period *and* the prior period, a strong sign of engagement and perceived product value. By far the most important—and hopefully largest—cohort.

▸ **Resurrected**: People who used the product at some time in the past—but not in the prior period—and have returned in the current period through reacquisition techniques. An audience that hangs in the balance as they may be as likely to depart for the long term as they are to stay. What can be done to keep them?

▶ **Churned**: People who used the product in the prior period but not in the current one, signaling a lack of perceived value or loss of access. (On a related note, it's a little known fact that Facebook routinely purges what it deems to be inauthentic accounts from Facebook, which is a significant user base price to pay—it has accounted for tens of millions of removed users over time—in order to maintain authentic identity across the service.)

Although the math may be simple, the moving pieces of cause and effect can quickly drown companies, so the Facebook team broke growth into three simple factors:

The North Star Metric: It's one thing to have data, it's another to be overwhelmed by it. To avoid endless navel-gazing or too many people chasing too many goals, Facebook selected a single metric that would be the subject of all their growth attention. The lingua franca for all teams—analytics, product, engineering and marketing—chipping away at The Wall.

For a company like AirBnB, this might be the number of nights booked on the service, for Uber the number of rides, for WhatsApp the number of messages sent, for eBay the amount of gross merchandise volume. It is the number that is to your service as gravity is to bowling. More inescapable and fundamental to success in the long term than any other.

For Facebook, that number would not be a Web 1.0 metric like page views or registered members. It would be engagement. The number of people who found enough value to use Facebook on a regular basis.

Over the years, Facebook would become increasingly sophisticated—and exacting—about the nature of engagement as they went from monthly active users (MAU) to daily active users (DAU), to the ratio of daily active users to monthly active users (DAU/MAU, a ludicrous 65% globally even to this day), to understanding the distribution of the frequency of people's usage over the past 28 days, to the number of people who used Facebook seven out of the past eight days (L7/8). They meticulously segmented their users into vintages (how long they had been on Facebook), engagement cohorts (how frequently they used it), demographics (their gender, age and location), methods and speed of access (desktop, smartphone, tablet, feature phone, 2G, 3G, LTE, broadband) and even psychographics (their actions and interests). They then carefully studied the differences and similarities in engagement among these co-horts, putting a special concentration on the "marginal" user who was not—yet—consistently engaged with Facebook.

When we talk about big data, *this* is what we mean.

The Magic Moment: It's good to have clarity on the outcome you're hoping to achieve, but what is the difference-maker that gets you there? The experience that gets people hooked on a product? The single most important thing that, if done well, causes you to grow and, if done poorly, destines you to irrelevance?

For Uber, the magic moment is the first time you push that button and a car shows up. For WhatsApp, it's the first message you send—often internationally—that doesn't incur an SMS or roaming charge. For AirBnB, it's that surprisingly lovely place with character in another city that doesn't feel like a hotel.

For Facebook, it was seeing your friends in your News Feed, so all efforts were aimed at getting you to that moment as fast as possible. Once it was clear how crucial this was to Facebook, it was all hands on deck to get you to seven friends within ten days of joining Facebook, then to ten friends in two weeks and to fifty friends as fast as possible after that. Nothing was more predictive of long-term engagement with Facebook—independent of your demographics or psychographics—than helping you make these connections as quickly as possible.

The Core Product Value: After getting people hooked via your Magic Moment, you have to deliver the day-in-and-day-out value that earns loyalty from your users. For Facebook, that is the feeling of connectedness people so consistently point to about the service, which is delivered most importantly by a great experience in the Facebook News Feed. Thank you, Chris Cox.

The rest was just blood, sweat and tears.

Inside Facebook's Growth Engine

Armed with their North Star Metric, Magic Moment and Core Product Value, the team got down to business. Under Palihapitiya's direction, there would be no ego and no lore. Just hard work and data: (1) get people to the front door, (2) have the Magic Moment as quickly as possible and (3) offer core product value as often as possible. Schultz and his team would focus on all things related to the front door—acquisition and resurrection and the data behind conversion and retention, Gleit on activation and the speed-to-Magic-Moment, and Olivan on one of the most significant product value evolutions in Facebook's history.

When it came to acquisition, Schultz's team wouldn't just use best-in-class search engine optimization and search engine marketing with significant budgets; they would broker a landmark deal with Google to allow the search engine giant to use its automated tools to read, store and make searchable the public parts of Facebook profiles—basics like your name and profile picture, which were not behind the walls of Facebook's privacy controls. This ensured that whenever you typed the name of a friend into Google, you'd be made aware—the vast majority of the time in the top search result—if they were on Facebook, driving increased interest in joining yourself.

Activating you on Facebook entails everything from the moment you first arrive at the home page to the process of signing up and your early moments on the site. The New User Experience—known affectionately as NUX inside Facebook—included the painstaking work of nailing the first few crucial moments of sign-up by building simple pages that depended on the careful testing—including eye-tracking studies—of every word, button, color and even page load speed. Every confusing direction, extra click and fraction of a second wasted threatened to destroy the work of getting a new user to this point.

Then came an important moment of truth on the way to the Magic Moment: importing your contacts from other services, especially e-mail providers like Hotmail, Yahoo, AOL and Gmail, to make connecting with friends of yours already on Facebook—and inviting those that were not yet—much more effortless. Contact importing came with a heaping of political intrigue as services like the e-mail providers had to allow Facebook access to retrieve users' contact lists through tools like application programmer interfaces (APIs), a classic example of co-opetition. In 2010, Facebook even acquired contact-importing technology provider Octazen who had a reputation both for building useful tools to help import contacts for the over 30% of Facebook's users who were not on one of the big e-mail platforms, as well as operating in gray areas obtaining contact information from public web pages of other services without using provided—and controlled—access methods, known as "scraping."

To understand the importance of contact importing to Facebook's growth, take a look at the math involved in creating virality in a business with so-called network effects like Facebook. To grow exponentially, you have to be able to translate one new user into a little more than one additional new user. If U is the original user and UF are the user's friends, it looks like this:

$$\text{Invites}_U \times \text{E-mail click rate}_{UF} \times \text{Facebook sign-up rate}_{UF} > 1$$

Here's an example: a user sends 100 invites to friends, those friends click on the invite 30% of the time, and those clickers complete the Facebook sign-up 5% of the time:

$$100 \times 30\% \times 5\% = 1.5$$

Presto, that first user is responsible for bringing 1.5 *new* users to Facebook.

Contact importers ensured that the first number in this equation was as high as possible. The way invite e-mails were composed controlled the second number, and the simplicity of the Facebook sign-up flow controlled the third. Even small changes in the individual components have a large compounding effect on the eventual outcome. Taking the same example a few steps further, if it went on with similar numbers for three "generations" of new users, it would look like this:

$$(100 \times 30\% \times 5\%) \times (100 \times 30\% \times 5\%) \times (100 \times 30\% \times 5\%) = 3.4$$

The first user would actually be responsible for bringing 3.4 people onto the platform. But if the number of invites in each case had been just 80 instead of 100 (or Facebook's sign-up conversion had been just 4% instead of 5%), it would have been just 1.7 people. Half as many. Powerful stuff!

For resurrection, Facebook relied on an old medium—e-mail—and a much older human motivation: curiosity. Resurrection targets were already users of Facebook with existing connections to friends, so sending the occasional e-mail to them about what their friends were doing—that new wall post or photo tag—created reasons to swing by Facebook if you hadn't in a while.

By using e-mail for friend invites and resurrection, Facebook became a master of using the medium they were replacing to feed the new medium they were creating.

More important than all of that, of course, was retention. Getting you beyond the first Magic Moment quickly and fortifying your engagement by delivering Core Product Value. To extend the contact importers' role in getting you to seven friends in 10 days, 10 friends in two weeks and 50 friends as soon as possible, in early 2008 Gleit and the team introduced the People You May Know feature—known internally as PYMK—that resided to the right of your growing News Feed. Pulled from a sophisticated combination of information from your imported contacts, your friends' friends with whom you share the most friends and commonality of work, college or interests, Facebook could determine a "friend distance" that allowed them to rank people you were not yet friends with but likely would want to be, and surface the most likely candidates for you. Conversely, as new friends joined Facebook and connected with you, Facebook would reach out to you to encourage you to suggest additional friends for the new user.

At the same time, Olivan and a team had been working on another big opportunity to deliver Core Product Value: translating Facebook into languages beyond English to increase the site's usability and appeal internationally. This wasn't as simple as translating the site into half a dozen common languages. It wasn't just that in countries like Germany, there were only 600,000 Facebook users even though there were over 40 million Internet users. There were hundreds of millions of Internet users in countries beyond the top 10 global languages.

Instead of moving a team of dozens into each prospective country and translating the site themselves, as MySpace was doing, or using just professional translations services, the Facebook team built an application on top of Facebook's own platform that allowed the site to be broken into its 300,000 component words and phrases and localized in a crowd-sourced way by letting target groups of Facebook users suggest—and vote on—local translations that would then be overseen by professional translators.

Using the technique, Facebook was able to launch its first translation—in Spain—in just two weeks, its German translation in two days, and its French translation in just 24 hours.

By the middle of 2008, they had 16 translations that would eventually grow to 20, overseen by professional translators and an additional 80 just crowd-sourced, creating loyalty from traditionally underrepresented communities such as Basque, Cherokee and Hausa.

The translations were a major contributor to a growth phenomenon Facebook had seen since its earliest days: early adopters of Facebook in a particular country would make the majority of their initial friend connections to *other* countries that had a more established Facebook user base. These were known as "exogenous" connections and implied a stronger comfort with non-native languages on the part of the early adopters. As translations became available in-country, the site became more inviting to primarily native speakers—the majority of that country's population—and as friend connections made between people continued to grow, the majority of those connections became "endogenous"—between people in the same country. In country after country, when that crossover from *exogenous* to *endogenous* connections came, Facebook user growth would kick into a new and sustained gear, signaling an acceptance beyond early adopters that cemented country-level engagement and loyalty over the long term.

The outcome of all the team's efforts in its first six months was much more than just interesting sociological phenomena: according to comScore, by June 2008—on the back of strong international results—Facebook had grown to 124 million users, accelerating past MySpace's global user base for the first time. A year later, in June 2009, Facebook finally exceeded MySpace's user base in that company's final stronghold, the United States, where Facebook had doubled in size to 70 million users in just one year and MySpace had declined by 5%.

Eighteen months of intense focus by the growth team had put MySpace behind them and proven that social networking is interesting to way more than 100 million people.

The Importance of Being Mobile

But if Facebook's *sine qua non* is retention and engagement, there would be no more important enabler—or inhibitor—of growth than the emergence of mobile as the world's favorite medium, which happened practically in its entirety within the lifetime of Facebook's growth team as less than 1.5 million iPhones had been sold by the time of the team's formation in late 2007.

In a world dominated by mobile, Facebook would have to become a daily—and preferably hourly—habit since, according to Forrester, people spend a giant 84% of all their time with apps in just five apps.

A simple first step of offering a mobile-optimized website at m.facebook.com came in 2007 and was followed throughout 2008 with native Facebook apps for Apple iOS, Blackberry, Windows Mobile and Nokia's Symbian, and finally in September 2009 for Google's Android, which had proven a more complex effort given the wide range of hardware and operating system versions for which an Android app has to work.

By February 2010, 25% of Facebook's 400 million monthly active users were accessing it over mobile, making it a good time to turn a much keener eye to how people engaged with Facebook in emerging markets where oftentimes broadband landline infrastructure had been skipped entirely in favor of a mobile one but where purchasing power lagged, making low-end phones and limited cellular speeds and data consumption prevalent.

In May of 2010, Palihapitiya announced the launch of Facebook Zero, a minimal text-only version of Facebook's service that would not accrue any cellular data charges on the networks of the 50 operators in 45 countries the service launched with. The intention was to extend the feeling of the basics of being connected via Facebook to many more people, some of whom would—having tasted some the value of Facebook and the Internet—steer more of their limited discretionary income toward cellular data plans with the providers offering Facebook Zero. Uptake of the service was rapid in certain regions—it is often credited with doubling the number of Facebook users in Africa over the course of only 18 months. Over time, however, the "zero rated" pricing of the service began to run into regulatory concerns around so-called net neutrality—the principle that all Internet traffic must be treated equally by operators—causing the offering to either be tightly restricted in duration or ended altogether. We'll see more about this complex issue in the story of Internet.org in Chapter 14.

About a year after the launch of Zero, Facebook addressed a different element of lower-end mobile infrastructures when Gleit traveled to Tel Aviv to acquire Israeli company Snaptu in March 2011. The company had developed a way for so-called feature phones—phones that had some data and messaging capabilities but lacked the sophistication of smartphones to run web browsers or apps—to access a basic version of Facebook. With the added functionality of Snaptu, Facebook was able to reduce the fraction of phones they could *not* address down to just 20%. After renaming the service Facebook for Every Phone, they grew it to 100 million monthly active users—nearly 10% of all Facebook users at the time—in the 18 months following the acquisition.

In June 2015, five years after launching their first emerging market mobile offering, Facebook combined all of its accumulated knowledge and technology into what will likely be the most important long-term offering for these markets, Facebook Lite.

Aimed at so-called typical Android phones that, according to analytics firm IDC, account for about two-thirds of the global smartphone market but have less performance and are connected to slower networks than your phone and mine, Lite uses a sophisticated combination of a lightweight app on the phone—a mere 1 MB, which is one-hundredth the size of Facebook's iOS app and downloads in about a minute even on 2G networks—coupled with a persistent and compressed connection to Facebook servers that do most of the heavy work of fetching content and formatting it for display on the phone in order to deliver a low-bandwidth experience that still feels very much like Facebook. By March 2016, just nine months after its launch, Facebook Lite became Facebook's fastest growing app ever as it reached 100 million users and counted critical markets like Brazil, India, Mexico, Indonesia and the Philippines among its top five heaviest users.

All the mobile effort has led to an amazing 90% of Facebook's users now accessing it via mobile, a complete inversion compared to desktop in just seven years. (See Figure 5-2.)

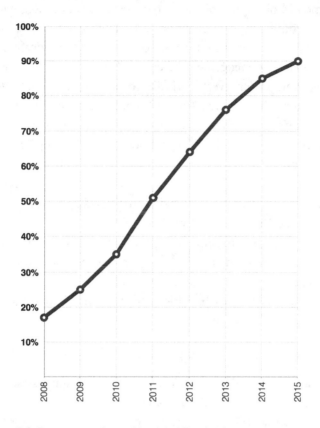

Figure 5-2. Percentage of monthly global Facebook users accessing via mobile[2]

The Outcomes of Wearing Overalls and Looking Like Hard Work

Thomas Edison is often credited with saying, "The reason a lot of people do not recognize opportunity is because it usually goes around wearing overalls looking like hard work." Edison would have liked Facebook.

When you walk through the areas belonging to the growth and internationalization teams in Facebook's cavernous offices today, you notice three things: dozens and dozens of flags representing countries all across the world, many different languages being spoken, and hard work in the form of monitors.

Lots of monitors.

Like some unholy union of Bloomberg terminals and hospital heart rate monitors built just for Facebook, they hang everywhere, and the teams meticulously observe country by country—and practically in real-time—the impact on engagement of every obscure local holiday, every broken contact importer, every periodic communist government shutdown in Vietnam, every launch—or end—of a mobile operator promotion, every rise or drop in the average review scores of its mobile apps, every little change in Facebook's product, even the impact of local weather. They do it because even a 1% difference in either direction is a big day.

What, then, has all this effort added up to? Good news, that's what.

In early 2016, eight years after the birth of the growth team, Facebook had grown to 1.59 billion monthly users—and 1 billion daily users, making it the leading social network in 129 countries (with Facebook's own Instagram in second place in 41 of those countries).[3]

Only four countries with Internet infrastructures had eluded Facebook's concerted winning pursuits:

> ▶ **China**: Facebook is currently blocked by the government.

> ▶ **Russia**: Local social network VKontakte—a blatantly stolen and localized version of Facebook—illegally offers premium TV, movie and music, keeping Facebook from picking up more than 15 million of the country's 105 million Internet users.

> ▶ **Japan**: Local messenger Line has roughly double Facebook's 30 million users.

> ▶ **South Korea**: Local messenger KakaoTalk has 15% higher penetration.

And what of Chamath, Javier, Alex and Naomi eight years later? Fear not. They are still plying their trade.

Palihapitiya left Facebook in 2011 to become part owner of the Golden State Warriors NBA franchise, occasional professional poker player and outspoken founder and CEO of the ascendant venture capital firm Social Capital Partnership, which has made growth marketing—with partners formerly from Facebook's growth team—one of the primary services it offers to its portfolio companies. Palihapitiya has become so influential that his is perhaps the only voice that could displace that of Marc Andreessen as the seer of things and speaker of truths among the new generation of venture capitalists. Or at least that's what Palihapitiya would have you believe.

Following Palihapitiya's departure, Olivan became the leader of all of Facebook's growth efforts, reporting directly to Zuckerberg and overseeing all growth-related products, marketing, analytics, data science, internationalization, Internet.org and Facebook's Social Good efforts.

Schultz now leads growth marketing and data science for not just Facebook's users but also its long tail of advertisers—as of September 2016 there were more than 4 million—and other Facebook products that can benefit from his team's expertise, including Messenger, which crossed its own 1 billion user milestone in July 2016. He has also become a leading light in the ranks of senior business leaders around the world active in support of the LGBT community.

And Gleit is now the second longest tenured Facebook employee after Zuckerberg himself and has ascended to lead all growth and engagement products after having been involved in everything from Facebook's New User Experience to People You May Know, privacy simplifications, tools to extend Facebook's experience to very low-end phones, the Follow feature and the Social Good capabilities including nonprofit donations tools that have facilitated millions of dollars in giving between people and organizations all over the world, and the Safety Check feature that Facebook turns on locally during disasters such as earthquakes to allow Facebook users to check themselves in as safe and to stay connected with family and friends around the world.

Looking Ahead:
The First Billion Were *Not* the Hardest

If the 1.59 billion people using Facebook every month represent the first 12 years of Facebook's mission to connect the world, what has to happen in the next 12?

Before Facebook looks to grow further, they have to *retain* all their current active users, as Alex and Chamath taught us in Growth Math 101. That means keeping a very close eye not just on the data of their own services but also on that of others in order to understand what it is that people most want to use to feel more connected. This is so important that in 2013, Facebook spent $180 million to acquire little-known Israeli mobile analytics company Onavo and proceeded to shutter their public-facing insights, retaining just for themselves the ongoing data on which mobile apps were being used on a daily basis—and how they were used—on millions of phones around the world. While it was Facebook's own platform data that would help Zuckerberg understand Instagram's growth and daily engagement and determine the value of having it be a part of the Facebook mission, it would be Onavo's data that allowed him to understand WhatsApp's growth and intense engagement prior to that acquisition. And it will be Onavo's data that allows him to keep a close eye on other international players like Line, KakaoTalk, QQ and WeChat, and those closer to home like Snapchat.

With the flanks covered, it's time to get on with growth. To get a clearer picture of Facebook's process for future growth, Table 5-1 shows an overview of their current global presence across regions overall and a few of the largest countries specifically. The left side of the table captures the current state of the three most important variables in Facebook's fate: country population, the degree to which the Internet is accessible to that population, and the degree to which those Internet users use Facebook. I've shaded the regions and countries where Internet or Facebook penetration is particularly high (darker shade) or low (lighter shade).

The right side of the table is a hypothetical growth-hacking "worksheet" that we'll get to a little later.

Getting to two billion monthly active users—a trend line using data from the last few years suggests this could happen as early as the end of 2017—and *far beyond* can be simplified into two simultaneous long-term pursuits.

1. Increasing Facebook penetration among existing Internet users: While there are 3.4 billion global Internet users,[4] there are only 1.59 billion monthly Facebook users. Not everyone, of course, will use Facebook every month, but many countries have not yet reached the nearly 70% usage rate Facebook enjoys in countries like the United States (190 million Facebook users out of 280 million Internet users).

	Population	Internet Penetration	Internet Users	Facebook Penetration (of Internet)	Facebook Users	Inc. FB: Winning FB Pen. (56%)	Inc. FB: Good FB Pen. (68%)	Inc. FB: Avg. Internet, FB Pen.	Inc. FB: Good Internet, FB Pen.	Inc. FB: Likely by 2022
Global	**7,260**	46%	3,340	48%	1,599	591	780	369	978	1,044
North America	**357**	**88%**	**314**	**68%**	**213**					
US	321	87%	281	68%	192					
Canada	36	93%	33	64%	21					
Latin America	**617**	**56%**	**345**	**86%**	**297**					
Brazil	204	58%	118	88%	103					
Mexico	122	49%	60	92%	55					
Colombia	48	59%	28	84%	24					
Argentina	43	80%	35	78%	27					
Europe and Middle East	**1,058**	**69%**	**727**	**49%**	**359**					
Russia	146	71%	103	11%	11	47	59			
Germany	81	88%	72	40%	29	5	20			5
Turkey	78	60%	46	89%	41					
France	66	84%	55	58%	32					
UK	65	92%	60	64%	38					
Italy	61	62%	38	74%	28					
Spain	46	77%	36	62%	22					
Africa	**1,158**	**29%**	**331**	**38%**	**125**					
Nigeria	182	51%	93	16%	15	37	48		73	73
Ehtiopia	99	4%	4	100%	4			42	67	42
Egypt	88	55%	48	56%	27					
Dem. Rep. Congo	79	3%	2	80%	2			27	43	27
South Africa	55	49%	27	48%	13		5		13	5
Tanzania	51	15%	8	36%	3		2	9	22	9
Kenya	45	71%	32	16%	5	13	17			13
Asia Pacific	**4,069**	**41%**	**1,649**	**32%**	**522**					
China	1,362	50%	674	0%	3	375	456			375
India	1,252	30%	376	36%	136	74	119	186	468	256
Indonesia	256	31%	78	100%	78			40	104	104
Pakistan	199	15%	29	79%	23			49	89	49
Bangladesh	169	32%	54	52%	28			16	54	16
Japan	127	91%	115	22%	25	39	53			39
Phillipines	110	43%	47	100%	47				31	31
Vietnam	94	50%	47	74%	35				15	

Table 5-1. Population, Internet penetration and Facebook penetration (millions, Q4 2015)

As we can see in the right part of the growth hacking worksheet, the biggest opportunity here would be for Facebook to reach an agreement in the longer term with the Chinese government to provide some sort of connectivity product to the 675 million people on the Internet in **China**. A "winning" Facebook penetration of around 56% would mean another 375 million users. Zuckerberg is prepared for this to be a patient, long-term engagement, and his learning of Mandarin and becoming a lecturer at Tsinghua University are just a part of this effort.

The next biggest opportunity after China is clearly **India,** where Facebook is the social networking leader but has only 136 million of 376 million Internet users as monthly active users, an upside of between 74 and 119 million additional users depending on penetration.

The next closest opportunity would be the three big **sub-Saharan** countries of Kenya, Nigeria and South Africa, where Facebook counts only 33 million active monthly users out of 150 million Internet users, leaving an opportunity for 50 to 70 million additional users.

Japan and **Germany** will need to continue to be a focus for increased penetration as Facebook lags there with only 22% and 40% penetration of Internet users, respectively. The two countries are 3rd and 4th in advertising spend in the world—after the United States and China—and Facebook will need to make sure they are increasingly the choice for being connected to people to show that it is a relevant personal influence in these markets.

While **Russia** also presents a significant population with healthy Internet connectivity, it has been hard for Facebook to grow beyond a small 11% share of that audience. Instagram is actually more popular in Russia, but the country promises to continue to stymie Facebook's overall efforts here.

2. Increasing Internet connectivity of the world's population: Only about 46% of the world's 7.3 billion people are on the Internet today, even though the fraction of people over age six in the world who have a mobile phone is projected to reach 90% by 2020.[5] The state of the infrastructure, cost of Internet access relative to discretionary income and even the awareness of and desire for the Internet are very real barriers in many places in the world.

In Asia (expected to be the region with 56% of *all* new smartphone subscriptions globally between 2016 and 2021 at 1.43 billion[6]), the Indian subcontinent (**India, Pakistan** and **Bangladesh**) and the Southeast Asian countries of **Indonesia, Philippines** and **Vietnam** present significant connectivity upside.

As can be seen in Table 5-1, infrastructure projects for India, Pakistan and Bangladesh that would lift Internet penetration anywhere from the global average of 46% all the way to 71% (similar to countries like Russia or Kenya) and Facebook penetration to between 56% and a high of 79% (in Pakistan) could add between 250 to 600 million users.

In Indonesia and the Philippines, where practically everyone with Internet access is on Facebook, and in Vietnam, where Facebook has 74% penetration, improved Internet penetration could add between 40 and 150 million users.

Another big connectivity opportunity are the nearly 50 countries in **sub-Saharan Africa**, which have a combined population of about 1 billion people but by far the world's weakest Internet penetration at less than 28%. It's obvious that these numbers would not escape a team as focused as Facebook's growth team. They're so focused on it, in fact, that together with Facebook's Connectivity Lab, they have partnered with European agency Eutelsat, Israeli satellite manufacturer Spacecom and U.S. satellite launch vehicle provider SpaceX—the first collaboration between Silicon Valley titans Zuckerberg and Elon Musk—to launch broadband satellite AMOS-6 in the second half of 2016 to provide coverage to 14 countries in that very region: Nigeria, Ethiopia, Democratic Republic of Congo, South Africa, Kenya, Tanzania, Uganda, Ghana, Cameroon, Cote d'Ivoire, Angola, Senegal, South Sudan and Gabon.

Together, the countries to be covered by the satellite represent a population of 670 million people, of which 202 million are on the Internet but only 54 million on Facebook.

If Internet connectivity could be improved to the world average or beyond, and assuming winning or better penetration for Facebook, it could mean an additional roughly 150 million to 300 million people connected via Facebook.

Table 5-2 shows the detailed numbers behind this sophisticated growth effort.

	Population	Internet Penetration	Internet Users	Facebook Penetration (of Internet)	Facebook Users	Inc. FB: Winning FB Pen. (56%)	Inc. FB: Good FB Pen. (68%)
Nigeria	182	51%	93	16%	15	32	73
Ehtiopia	99	4%	4	100%	4	42	67
Dem. Rep. Congo	79	3%	2	80%	2	27	43
South Africa	55	49%	27	48%	13	1	13
Tanzania	51	15%	8	36%	3	10	22
Kenya	45	71%	32	16%	5	7	17
Uganda	37	32%	12	15%	2	8	16
Ghana	26	19%	5	58%	3	4	10
Cameroon	24	11%	3	54%	1	5	10
Cote d'Ivoire	23	23%	5	35%	2	4	9
Angola	20	25%	5	66%	3	3	6
Senegal	14	50%	7	24%	2	2	5
South Sudan	12	16%	2	8%	0	3	6
Gabon	2	39%	1	54%	0	0	0
TOTAL	669		205		55	148	297

Table 5-2. Intended AMOS-6 satellite coverage country population, Internet penetration and Facebook penetration (millions, Q4 2015)

As if to illustrate both the very real risks of increasing connectivity around the world *and* Zuckerberg's imperviousness to them, as this book went into production in September 2016 the first instantiation of the AMOS-6 satellite was the victim of a catastrophic explosion of a SpaceX Falcon rocket on its launch pad at Cape Canaveral Air Force Station while being fueled ahead of a test firing the day before the satellite's launch. Zuckerberg, who was in Africa at the time to celebrate the satellite's anticipated arrival in space, was undaunted in his update on Facebook following the incident:

> As I'm here in Africa, I'm deeply disappointed to hear that SpaceX's launch failure destroyed our satellite that would have provided connectivity to so many entrepreneurs and

everyone else across the continent. Fortunately, we have developed other technologies like Aquila that will connect people as well. We remain committed to our mission of connecting everyone, and we will keep working until everyone has the opportunities this satellite would have provided.

Perhaps even more telling was Zuckerberg's reply to a commenter who asked what the insurance costs of a satellite were: "The problem isn't the money; it's that now it may take longer to connect people."

Certainly Zuckerberg is committed, but the satellite's demise makes abundantly clear that none of this will be easy. Contrary to popular opinion, the pursuit of connecting emerging markets is not a Machiavellian revenue grab by Zuckerberg. Connecting these markets is both more expensive and less lucrative than established markets like the United States—they monetize at less than one-tenth the level per user today.

If Zuckerberg were obsessed only with the return of every dollar he spent today, he would *not* be putting satellites in orbit. It's just the continuation of the world's most deliberate growth engine in the service of a mission to connect the world, and in about five years, just the examples I've covered could represent an additional billion users for Facebook.

6

How Facebook Built a $10 Billion Business in Three Years

LESSON 4:

***Everybody wins if you democratize
something for customers of all sizes.***

Background: One of the most important aspects of an increasingly connected world is that it allows more providers and more customers to participate in all systems. When perfectly harnessed, this capability can create more powerful services for smaller providers, better choices for consumers and larger customer bases for even the biggest providers.

Facebook's Move: Facebook introduced advertising in its wildly popular News Feed backed by an auction system—similar to Google's—that made the system accessible to advertisers of all sizes, ensured the best possible content was matched to the best possible people to drive strong business results, rewarded high-quality advertisers and punished low-quality ones.

Thought Starter: What process are you democratizing?

The Sheryl Sandberg of 2007 was an unlikely business partner for the Mark Zuckerberg of the same model year. Zuckerberg a 23-year-old coder with a growing—but not leading—social media service making roughly $100 million annually. Sandberg a proven, late thirty-something star of government (chief of staff for Clinton-era U.S. Secretary of Treasury Larry Summers) and business (VP of the largest part of Google's advertising business) who oversaw roughly $10 billion in annual revenue.

The only thing they had in common was attending Harvard, although Sandberg was awarded the John H. Williams Prize as top graduating economics student while Zuckerberg quit in his sophomore year.

Never underestimate the power of dinner and a mission.

Over a number of one-on-one meals at Sandberg's house in late 2007 and early 2008, the mission to make the world more open and connected, which Zuckerberg had so unrelentingly been pursuing, won her over to becoming chief operating officer of Facebook. Perhaps the only thing better than the "rocket ship" working on organizing the world's *information* and making it universally accessible, which then CEO of Google Eric Schmidt had convinced Sandberg to join in 2001, was the rocket ship working on organizing the world's *people* and making them universally accessible, which Zuckerberg was encouraging her to join. That, and the fact that there was no room for a COO in the traffic jam of leadership at the top of Google made up of Schmidt and cofounders Larry Page and Sergey Brin.

To celebrate, Zuckerberg gave Sandberg the hardest job in Silicon Valley.

Win–Lose: A Brief History of Advertising

Although the most basic forms of oral and written advertising date back as far as many centuries B.C.E. and range as far and wide as China, India, Rome, Greece and Egypt, the Industrial Revolution is chiefly responsible for the rise of advertising as a giant industry.

Before large-scale, centralized manufacturing (e.g., Procter & Gamble, Gillette, Levis), national retailing (e.g., Wanamaker's, Macy's, Sears Roebuck) and advanced transportation systems for distribution became prevalent in the mid- to late-1800s, you understood and bought goods from your local shopkeeper whom you knew personally and who concocted, procured and explained these goods for you.

With the vanishing of the shopkeeper, however, the function of making you aware of, getting you to prefer and finally transacting a good or service had to scale up just as manufacturing and distribution had. Welcome to the golden age of advertising, and with it the age of mass media—first the newspaper, then radio, then television and eventually the Internet.

And if you feel that advertising has been to varying degrees intrusive, you would be right. It's right there in the Latin root of the word *advertere*, to "turn toward."

It makes you turn extra pages in magazines and newspapers, makes you wait for your radio traffic report, gives you a chance to go to the bathroom during the Super Bowl and keeps you from reading the front page of ESPN's website.

Getting you "turning toward" a product or service is so vital—and in some cases even effective—that over $600 billion a year are spent globally on various forms of advertising.

However, hanging—like a musty blanket—over the entire advertising business is the sense that it has never shaken the win–lose nature of the interaction between people and businesses, especially when it comes to digital advertising:

▸ **When advertisers win, people lose**: If a media provider can do a great job of getting you to turn toward advertising—especially true for the Internet's so-called home page takeovers that obscure the content for which you came to sites like Yahoo, ESPN and CNN—people have at best a sense of disruption and at worst a deep resentment. Yes, they are getting content for free, but as they increasingly vote with their wallets to support ad-free services like Netflix, it becomes clear that free won't always be a winning price.

▸ **When people win, advertisers lose**: When a service is most useful to people—take Google search as a prime example—advertisers feel constrained in their ability to communicate via the small, text-only ads served up with people's search results. Advertisers—and the hundreds of thousands of people that work at the agencies tasked with making their advertising clients successful—hate not being able to express themselves visually. The only thing they dislike more is not being able to create interest in their product where there was none before—nearly 90% of advertising is spent on so-called demand generation—and if people don't type "red crayon" into Google search, "red crayon" companies are out of luck when it comes to digital's biggest advertising tool to date.

▸ **Mostly, everybody loses:** There are many, many corners of the digital advertising world where both advertisers and people lose because experiences are polluted with ads that are ineffective for the advertiser *and* disruptive to people. Billions of these impressions are served every day in the gutters of the digital world.

Mission Impossible?

But that was merely the beginning.

Sandberg wasn't just shackled by advertising's 150-year win–lose history. At Facebook, she was tasked with building a large advertising business in a product culture that was obsessively people-first. Zuckerberg, chief product officer Chris Cox and their teams keenly understood that Facebook's success bringing people to the service and keeping them engaged came from pushing Facebook's minimalist design to the background to allow the people and things that mattered to them to come to the foreground. It was Facebook's prime directive to keep it that way.

There was only one thing worse for the company than interfering with user experience, and to make for a perfect storm, Sandberg would have to navigate it as well: peoples' concerns about privacy juxtaposed with the opportunity of Facebook's advertising to leverage the billions of daily pieces of information that real people—well over 90% of Facebook accounts are believed to be authentic—share with friends about their lives.

Sandberg, however, was undaunted. She is a serious operator with the finely tuned impatience to avoid every great company's worst fate: poor execution. In that, she reminded me—in the best ways—of the patron saint of all great Silicon Valley operators, former Intel CEO Andy Grove. Sandberg stepped into the moment and throughout the first half of 2008 worked across all parts of the company—Cox in particular would become a close friend and confidant—and reached consensus on advertising as the central business model of Facebook's future.

However, the early days of Facebook's efforts showed clearly just how complicated the situation would be.

Before she could even concentrate on advancing the advertising products built by Facebook specifically for Facebook, she had to extract the company from an agreement struck with Microsoft the year before her arrival to show banner ads from Microsoft's ad network on Facebook. The theory had been that Facebook brought additional inventory to Microsoft's network while Microsoft could handle portions of ad sales for a fledgling Facebook, but it had become clear that serving the Microsoft ads was inconsistent with the nature of Facebook and took inventory Facebook wanted to use for ads targeted and delivered by its own systems. Extracting themselves from the obligation—a feat handled deftly by Sandberg's vice president of corporate development Dan Rose—was a tenuous bit of work, as the deal had been part of Microsoft's $240 million investment in Facebook in 2007, which had valued the company at $15 billion.

Managing just its own advertising products brought focus and reasonable revenue growth for Facebook in 2009 and 2010 from the handful of ads stacked vertically on the right-hand side of nearly every page of their browser-based experience. They were targeted to users based on basic Facebook information such as age, location and stated interests and priced to charge advertisers only when users clicked on the ads. That success, however, quickly brought the seedy underbelly of Internet advertising to Facebook: so-called affiliates who opportunistically roam the Internet frontier like mercenaries in search of opportunities to drive clicks to their clients in make-a-fast-buck enterprises, especially in the second tier of the dieting and dating industries. Facebook soon filled with ads featuring "muffin top" waistlines and women in questionable attire.

By the end of 2010—three years into Sandberg's efforts—Facebook's business was profitable but stuck between a rock and a hard place.

The rock of Facebook users who disliked low-quality ads, and the hard place of higher-quality advertisers, like national and global brands and the local businesses that people cared about, not moving their advertising to Facebook. Who wants to live in a neighborhood with the broken fences and dried-up lawns of dieting and dating? Besides, Facebook's existing ads were widely thought too small and unproven for outcomes beyond mid-tier online e-commerce.

Imagine a meeting with the head of a movie studio looking to show beautiful trailer videos complaining about Facebook's postage stamp–sized picture ads, and you get an idea of what Sandberg's days looked like.

To make matters worse, the cognoscenti in the industry had begun to whisper and wonder what Sandberg would do if the mobile wave—which had begun in earnest with the arrival of the iPhone in 2007—became a tsunami. As Facebook's own advertising product leader at the time, Greg Badros, would point out, there is no room for ads on the "right-hand side" of a phone. That's where your hand is.

And pressure from the outside was mounting. Private investments in January of 2011 valued Facebook at $50 billion, putting more pressure on the business to grow the way perennial Internet advertising role model Google had at a similar stage in its life cycle. In 2004, Google's 6th full year of operation, they had generated nearly $3.2 billion. In its 6th full year of operation, Facebook lagged by nearly half, having generated less than $2 billion.

Sandberg was, quite literally, chasing her past.

In the Meantime:
A Giant Medium in the Making

While Sandberg was wrestling with the business, things on the user side were all sunshine. From 2008 through 2010, Facebook had grown its global user base nearly 10 times to over 600 million monthly active users while retaining nearly two-thirds of that number as daily users, an almost unheard-of level of user engagement. It wasn't just that Facebook had long left MySpace in the dust. According to comScore, the end of 2010 marked Facebook's ascent to the top spot in the United States for total time spent by Internet users, eclipsing the various offerings of former leaders Yahoo and Google.

Chiefly responsible for this degree of success with people was the central and most used feature of Facebook: the News Feed.

Launched toward the end of 2006 by Cox and his team, the News Feed was your personalized daily newspaper, featuring the people and things that mattered to you. Courtesy of its famous algorithm, which reduced the average of 1,500 daily pieces of information generated by your network of connections down to the 150 that it estimated mattered most and would be shown to you, News Feed was a seemingly endless river of everything from the sublime and profound to the banal. It never ran out, and, whether by value or compulsion, you could never be away from it for very long.

Facebook's News Feed may have started as a mere feature, but by the end of 2010 it was well on its way to becoming one of the greatest media ever as it increasingly became the lens through which we observe our world. That is to say, our friends and the things we chose to connect to had become our editors. It was Facebook's greatest triumph relative to its mission of making the world more open and connected.

As of the end of 2015, News Feed was delivering over 200 million of its stories to people around the world every minute. And in the year that people's time using mobile overall eclipsed that of all time spent watching television, Facebook and Instagram together were the mobile attention champions, accounting for one in every five minutes spent on mobile, the vast majority of which involved looking at the respective feeds.

At first blush, it would appear that News Feed was the obvious answer to Sandberg's advertising challenge: larger ads that confer to advertisers the same ability to express themselves as News Feed does to people who liberally shared pictures (and in later years video) placed in the middle of the most important consumer stream of information in all of digital—if not in all of media of any kind. But, since the end of early advertising experiments in News Feed in 2007, no ads had appeared in that hallowed ground. The ad business was a raft in the ocean of News Feed. Water, water everywhere, but not a drop to drink.

Some product purists within the company entirely rejected the notion of ads in News Feed. Zuckerberg, Sandberg and Cox, however, knew that the answer was more nuanced. That they had to aim for a future—independent of how long it would take to achieve—where ads in News Feed were seen as equally valuable to content from friends or things people were connected to. That could happen only if the best possible ad had been chosen for the best possible person, a problem with two sides: understanding people to an unprecedented extent and having enough advertising to choose from for each person to make the best connection.

And so the intersection of ads and News Feed would become the most important existential question Facebook had ever faced. Did they have enough information, enough advertisers and advertising and enough experience to deliver the right content to the right person?

Would they risk their single most important asset? Could they survive in the long term if they didn't?

On the Threshold

The year 2011 would be a time of soul-searching for Zuckerberg, Sandberg and the teams working on the consumer and advertising products. Were they peanut butter and chocolate, or oil and water? Better together, or destined to be apart?

How could they possibly think about the huge risk of combining people's chosen content from friends and things they had connected to—known as "organic" content—and ads—"paid" content—in one very important column? How would you feel if the announcement of your best friend's firstborn was followed by an ad for teeth whitener?

It had been done successfully at the scale Facebook was contemplating only once. By Google, the juggernaut of digital advertising—and largest company by revenue in the entire global advertising business—who combined paid and organic items in a single search result page. That page was served in response to a search by the user, making combined organic and paid results dedicated to the expressed intent seem vaguely like the Yellow Pages of old, an experience people were familiar with and valued to a degree. Facebook, however, was aiming for something bigger and more complicated as it would have to show ads without the expressed intent Google's search provided. It would have to essentially divine the best possible ad.

Two difficult things would need to come together for Facebook to make that possible.

People and businesses would need to feel that they were on an equal footing when it came to content in the News Feed. A consistent appearance—albeit with ads identified as "Sponsored"—that would give businesses the opportunity to share photos and links just as people could and the same opportunity to pass by an ad with the same ease of flicking your thumb over a dull political post from your oversharing friend.

And people needed to feel that an ad had been selected for them as carefully as possible, both to deliver a good user experience and to improve efficacy for the advertiser, the only way Facebook's business could thrive in the long term.

The ads would have to be nearly as useful, interesting or entertaining as something from a friend or chosen connection.

In exchange for accessing an unparalleled degree of information people had shared about themselves, Facebook and the advertiser would have to do the best possible job of adding some kind of value.

The information assets at Facebook's disposal to achieve that were formidable. Not only did they have billions of daily signals on Facebook—mostly in the form of what people "liked" and posted on Facebook—but they had also become increasingly effective at augmenting this data with useful data from elsewhere. Chief among them the ability for businesses of all sizes to match their existing customers—through e-mails or phone numbers—to people on Facebook so that those businesses could more intelligently address their communication to existing customers, customers with certain profiles and behaviors or noncustomers. This was further extended by understanding other websites people visited and data from third-party data providers who could bring understanding of information like household-level motor vehicle records to aid in understanding car ownership and buying intention, grocery store shopping information, household income and family composition. All of these were made available to advertisers at an aggregated level that prevented the identification and targeting of any single person but provided the additional insight necessary to communicate more thoughtfully with people. And once advertisers found success with a particular target of consumers, they could simply ask Facebook to use its incredible depth of understanding to automatically find more people like the original group. Called "look-alike targeting," the technology uses *every* piece of data Facebook has on people to mathematically judge their similarity to the original cohort, going far beyond the basics of demographics a human advertiser would use and becoming one of the single most powerful tools in Facebook's arsenal for both advertisers and people.

You only have to look to the Super Bowl to understand the power of being more thoughtful: at any one time in the United States, only about 7 million people are in the market for a new pickup truck, but due to the broadcast nature of television, all 115 million viewers of the game have to endure the inevitable Ford F150 commercial. There is a famous quote about advertising by department store magnate John Wanamaker who said, "Half of my advertising is wasted. I just don't know which half." The truth, it turns out, is that the situation in advertising is most likely worse. In our Super Bowl truck example, more like 90% of the advertisers' investment—which totals a whopping $4.5 million for 30 seconds—is wasted. Facebook's premise to both people and advertisers was that it could invert this inefficiency for both parties. On Facebook, the truck advertiser would be able to have similar reach directly into that group of 7 million intenders as the Super Bowl but would likely waste no more than 10% of their advertising.

In the end, the answer to these two challenges, and whether ads in Facebook's News Feed could work, lay deep below the surface of the Facebook experience that you and I see and happens billions of times every day.

Each of these moments is the decision to show one ad to one person. And each of those decisions is made by a sophisticated algorithm that auctions the opportunity to communicate with that person to the most qualified ad and advertiser in Facebook's system as assessed by a combination of predicting the likely outcome of the ad being shown to that person based on the advertiser's and the person's history on Facebook, with the price each advertiser has bid to secure the attention of that person.

Imagine putting a slice of your attention up on an easel at an auction house and the fast-talking auctioneer selling it to the highest bidder from among a group of well dressed, prequalified advertisers including your local dentist and restaurant, your favorite online retailer and an athletic clothing manufacturer and automaker competing with your incumbent favorites.

It's like that. Billions of times a day. For every ad on Facebook.

This is not a new concept. It's how Google auctions its search result slots for words that users have typed into the search engine to advertisers bidding on those words. Just type "new car" into Google to see the advertiser food-fight in your paid search results.

What Facebook is doing, however, is more extensive. They are finding and auctioning a match between people and advertisers across much more than just keywords. That is partly to make the most of the data they have and differentiate from Google, but, more importantly, it is what's required to make the ads-in-News-Feed experience work.

Aside from finding a good match between advertiser and people, selecting each ad as an auction has other nice benefits. These include the leveling of the playing field between giant advertisers and smaller local advertisers. Each advertiser can get access to just the part of Facebook's user base most relevant to them, and each bids what the attention of those people is worth to them. Your local small business has the same opportunity to communicate with you as a national or global business spending literally thousands of times more money in aggregate.

Additionally, since prior performance indicators about each advertiser play a modifier role in the auction—higher performing advertisers as judged by inputs like historical user engagement and low negative response rates essentially get a discount in the auction, while lower performing ones are charged a premium—the auction is able to effectively price less effective advertisers out. Once ads for these advertisers become too expensive for their taste, they either work harder to improve their advertising or leave the auction, either way eliminating opportunities to sour people's experience.

Reward the thoughtful. Punish the thoughtless.

So, with just barely enough information and confidence, Zuckerberg and Sandberg made the most important decision in Facebook's existence.

They started to experiment with early versions of ads in the web-based Facebook News Feed in December 2011, opened more widely throughout the spring of 2012 and allowed the first ads in the mobile News Feed of the wildly popular Facebook iOS and Android mobile apps in July of 2012.

As these advertising dials were turned up, Facebook closely monitored the sentiment in its user surveys—they do as many as 50,000 a day—around the perceived quality of the Facebook News Feed. Lo and behold, the introduction of advertising had only a negligible effect.

Slowly but surely, they were conquering the impossible: a win–win solution for advertising.

A Win–Win[5] Solution

Looking at Facebook's advertising business a mere three years later, it's not just on the way to being a win–win, but likely a five-way victory:

▸ **It's good for people *and* advertisers**: By working hard aesthetically and technically to match the best ad to the best person, Facebook has made some of the most significant strides in the advertising industry ever. All the while, it has held itself accountable both to advertisers for the performance of its ads as well as to the sentiment of its users about those ads in their News Feed. Although difficult to summarize across advertiser industries and objectives, when used thoughtfully with creative executions that match the interests of its target audiences, Facebook advertising in News Feed—and especially on mobile and using video— routinely performs above the digital display marketing norms for reach, ad recall, brand awareness and return on investment maintained by industry observer Nielsen,[1] has lower cost-per-thousand impressions (CPM) and cost-per-click (CPC) than Twitter,[2] is considered by 95.8% of advertisers to produce the best return on investment (ROI) of all social media platforms[3] and is cited widely by businesses with direct marketing objectives (conversion) for beating Google via look-alike targeting.

▸ **It's good for creating awareness *and* transaction**: The process of communicating and engaging with people important to your business is often reduced to the conceptual model of a funnel with consumers going through various states of increasing attention to your business (awareness to consideration to preference to transaction to loyalty). Most advertising media have a tendency to have a particular strength at different points of this funnel. Television is more often used at the "top" of the funnel (e.g., the glamour shot of that new car or the fact that you can save 15% on car insurance), while direct mail or search is used almost exclusively at the bottom (e.g., 25% off sweaters at Target this weekend, buy this TV at amazon.com now). Facebook, however, has increasingly become a solution throughout the funnel to accommodate many advertisers with different objectives (e.g., Burberry would like you to prefer their brand of clothing, while hotels.com would much rather you make a reservation tonight), as well as providing a nearly complete solution for advertisers that prefer to operate throughout the funnel (e.g., Southwest Airlines, Mercedes).

▸ **It's good for large-scale *and* specific targeting**: Until Facebook, most advertisers had to make a Sophie's Choice between reaching people at large scale (e.g., Coke, Walmart) in media like television or web portals like Yahoo or with refined targeting (e.g., Michael Kors, Etsy) in much lower-reach media like magazines or lifestyle-specific websites. With Facebook, advertisers no longer have to choose as they enjoy access to extremely sophisticated targeting across a giant audience of 1 billion people a day. In the United States, for example, Facebook sees a Super Bowl worth of people. Every day. On mobile alone.

▸ **It's good for large advertisers *and* small**: The democratizing effect of the ad auction—and the opening of Facebook's advertising engine to outside providers who help advertisers take advantage of Facebook's tools and build additional capabilities on top of those tools (via a so-called Application Programmer Interface, or API)— creates opportunities for advertisers of all sizes, causing the ranks of monthly active Facebook advertisers to grow to 4 million as of September 2016. A very long tail that has a powerful diversifying effect on Facebook revenue, inoculating it against potential weakness in any individual advertiser objective, sector or region. More advertisers also means more advertising to choose from for each person. And the constant growth of Facebook users around the world means more options for each advertiser. All of which creates a system of growing both advertisers and people that only gets better the bigger it gets, which has caused even the largest and highest-quality advertisers in the world—finally convinced of Facebook's quality and efficacy—to come aboard. So long diets and dating!

▸ **It's good for traditional digital *and* mobile**: Remember those whispers in the industry about how Zuckerberg and Sandberg would deal with the mobile tsunami? Those are gone, replaced with the awed respect of Facebook having created the most envied mobile advertising solution in the industry. An endless feed of organic and paid content, perfect for phones and controlled by people's thumbs. It's so good that it's been proven to successfully augment the granddaddy of all advertising—television—for even the world's biggest advertisers.

It's Not All Clear Sailing Ahead

As successful as Facebook's moves in advertising have been, they had still only netted them a number two position behind Google by 2016. Challenges still lie ahead, the hardest of which is a direct outcome of their success.

If Facebook sells out its ad inventory, doesn't grow users faster than advertiser interest, does not show more content per person and isn't willing to increase its "ad load"—the ratio of organic content to paid content a user sees, which has historically hovered at roughly 10:1—the economics of supply and demand in its auctions will cause prices to rise for all advertisers, slowly making advertising on Facebook less attractive.

There are a number of potential ways to address this challenge, starting with making each individual ad on Facebook more effective—and thus worth more. That's the reason for the new ad types that Facebook has already introduced, including video and 360-degree video, multiunit horizontally scrolling Carousels and longer-form interactive Canvas ads—derived from Facebook's Instant Articles technology—which you can open directly in the News Feed and which have proven very engaging in the early going. All introduced for advertisers only after the same content was made available and successful for people to share.

Two forms of improving ad inventory are next on the strategic to-do list for Facebook. The first is to make existing inventory work harder. While inventory in key regions like North America and much of Europe is selling out at increasingly higher rates, opportunities to sell even more of their inventory at even higher value still exist elsewhere. Facebook's average revenue per user in North America is triple that of Europe and nearly 10 times that of the rest of the world. Much of that is due naturally to the lower value of the advertising industry in markets with less developed economies and therefore consumers with less—often substantially less—disposable income. Facebook is specifically building advertising products appropriate to regions with slower mobile infrastructures and even purposely slowing down the network on their own campus in Menlo Park every Tuesday to engender empathy among employees with consumers in precisely these markets.

The second is to add inventory, already underway in the form of ads appearing on Facebook's 2012 acquisition, Instagram, as well an ever expanding collection of web and mobile properties owned by others, called the Audience Network, where Facebook's ad technology is matching users and serving ads and sharing the resulting revenue. At more than 600 million monthly users as of December 2016, Instagram has grown to be larger than Twitter in terms of users and much larger than Twitter in terms of people's time spent, which correlates directly to amount of content—and therefore also ads—consumed. Using the same cautious playbook and underlying technology Facebook employed for ads in the News Feed of its namesake property, they are already having tremendous success growing advertising revenue in the similar medium of the Instagram feed.

Beyond that lies the challenge—and opportunity—of opening up a vein of revenue untapped by Facebook to date that would aim directly at the heart of Google: Facebook's version of search and search advertising. Search advertising in 2015 is a $80 billion global business—with Google taking a $45 billion lion's share—and is estimated by eMarketer to grow to $130 billion globally by 2019. Google's product and business are among the best ever devised, which explains why Sandberg and Zuckerberg are taking their time to determine whether Facebook could offer a better solution and, if so, how to prioritize the development effort relative to the products they are already building. Although it would require a complex interplay of trillions of pieces of information on the open Internet and trillions of pieces of information available only inside Facebook and a dash of as yet undeveloped artificial intelligence to structure people's free-form posts and comments on Facebook into something as easily searched as the open Internet's pages and links, a better product than Google's search is plausible. But expect Sandberg and Zuckerberg and some of the most advanced technical teams within Facebook to show patience, making an advanced Facebook search function with related advertising opportunities unlikely before 2018 at the earliest. Its arrival would launch a revenue food fight of unprecedented proportions between Google and Facebook.

But What a Grand Ship It Is

Challenges aside, the momentum of Facebook's advertising offerings is undeniable. As of the third quarter of 2015, they had 1 billion daily users. Annual ad revenue since the decision to put ads in Facebook's News Feed had quadrupled, with an outsized 80% of that revenue coming from ads in mobile news feeds as of the 4th quarter of 2015, a business they had grown from $0 to more than $10 billion annually in less than three years.

While there are already 4 million active advertisers as of September 2016 (a mere six months after having announced 3 million advertisers), the total number of businesses that have a presence on Facebook via its Pages product exceeded 60 million globally as of July 2016, all of them potential future paying customers with an increasing array of offerings from advertising on Facebook, Instagram and the Audience Network to future customer engagement and e-commerce tools on Messenger and WhatsApp.

The good news is slated to continue with industry observer eMarketer estimating that 2016 marked the year spending on digital advertising in the U.S. surpassed spending on television and that by 2019 mobile advertising spending will double its share of the total global advertising pie to nearly $200 billion annually, with Facebook Inc.—meaning Facebook and Instagram—taking nearly $40 billion of that and projected to be the leader in nonsearch advertising. Facebook has clearly skated to where the puck was going.

Sandberg has taken the hardest job in Silicon Valley, built on what she learned at Google—selling to advertisers of all sizes a product that integrates paid ads with organic content—and, together with Zuckerberg and the Facebook product teams, fashioned an even more powerful ad product able to serve more needs of more advertisers over the long term.

While Google will likely continue as the bigger of the two over a five-year horizon, Facebook has the trajectory and opportunities to outpace them beyond that.

Turns out Sandberg and Zuckerberg had been right during all those dinner conversations back in 2008: the only thing more powerful—for both people and advertisers—than organizing the world's information is organizing the world's people.

7

How Facebook Goes Fast

This is the story of how to build a cloud. A very big cloud.

Remember Chamath, Javier, Alex and Naomi and the Facebook growth team? Their focus in 2008 and 2009 to bring new users to Facebook *really* paid off inasmuch as they doubled the size of the service in each of those years (see Figure 7.1).

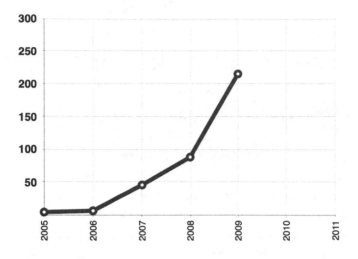

Figure 7-1. New Facebook monthly users (millions)

Heading into 2010, Facebook was staring down the barrel of the very real possibility of having to handle as many *additional* users in the year ahead as they had added to the service the first five and half years. All while *each* user was sharing more content than ever before.

The mysteries of how to make that happen are modern marvels and happen completely out of sight in something we've simply come to call "the cloud."

Industrial Revolution → Information Revolution → Facebook Revolution

At the dawn of the 19th century, the Industrial Revolution was in full swing, its belching trains and factories upending the way *things* were made and distributed. At the time, the "technologies" of efficient steam engines, advanced metallurgy and power looms were a mystery to most people, and the workers who made it all possible were nameless, faceless cogs in a very literal machine.

Two hundred years later, at the dawn of the 21st century, the Information Revolution was also very much in full swing. Networks were its trains, and computers its factories, and they changed the way *information* was made and distributed. Its technologies of fiber optics, data centers and millions of lines of code were many times more sophisticated than those of the Industrial Revolution, but most people not only did not understand them, they couldn't even *see* them or, for that matter, the people wrangling them.

Facebook, of course, is part of that Information Revolution, but—with apologies to *Spinal Tap*—"they have to go to 11" compared to the other guys. That personalized newspaper Chris Cox has been parenting for a decade? Turns out it's *very* complicated when you have to deliver it to a billion people all over the world on tens of thousands of different devices every day, often dozens of times for each person.

To deliver a Web 1.0 portal like Yahoo circa 1996—which had a directory of links to other sites and Reuters news articles—you had to store one source of stuff and then send that stuff to the tens of millions of people who clicked on it. No algorithms. No personalization.

With the emergence of search—and especially Google—things got more complicated. To create a map of the Internet, Google's computers have to constantly "crawl" the giant network and index its contents so that when you arrive looking for "When is the season 7 premiere of *Game of Thrones*?" it could use its algorithm to point you on your way to Westeros. The billion of us that use Google's PageRank search algorithm represent a huge advance in scale, sophistication and speed over portals, but we all search the same source and basically get the same answer to that *Game of Thrones* question. (I'll confess to slight oversimplification here since Google results are somewhat personalized taking into consideration country and locale of search and some degree of prior search history.)

Your Facebook News Feed, however, is entirely personal to you: *your* friends and things *you've* connected to, *their* content, *everyone's* privacy settings, and what interests *you* the most.

It takes a hundred servers in multiple locations and tens of thousands of pieces of data from objects and associations in different databases to assemble and deliver—in about a second—*your* personal newspaper.

In the age of mobile and short attention spans, Facebook knows you don't care how complicated all that is. Just that speed is a feature. And they work on every millisecond.

Table 7-1 compares the relative complexity of the key players in the Information Revolution.

	Number of Things	Size of Things	Number of Sources	To Number of People	Algorithm?
Early Yahoo	Medium	Small	one	100's of millions	—
Netflix	Small	Huge	one	10's of millions	Simple
YouTube	Billions	Big	millions	over a billion	Simple
Google Search	Trillions	Small	one	over a billion	Complicated
WhatsApp	Billions	Small	over a billion	over a billion	—

Table 7-1. Scale and complexity of delivering various Internet services

Facebook has come a long way from its humble beginnings when they grew the site infrastructure by one leased server—for $85 a month—every time they added a few tens of thousands of students.

Today—and every day—they serve over a billion people, deliver hundreds of billions of individual stories, collect over ten billion likes, comments and shares and more than a billion photos that require a few petabytes of new storage—that's a billion million or a giga mega—*per day*, and many exabytes of storage for all pictures ever uploaded.

Facebook has to store, understand the complex relationships between and deliver on a moment's notice many trillions of things, all the while protecting them from nuisances as small as spam and as complex as state-sponsored cyber attacks.

No wonder, then, that by 2015, Facebook owned $3.6 billion of equipment and $3.9 billion of land and buildings and was investing $4.8 billion per year on the engineers that create and manage these systems.

All of those engineers and assets make possible that quick glance at your Facebook News Feed, your Instagram or your Messenger while in line at Starbucks. It's more complicated than the Information Revolution of even just 10 years ago, and we don't know how it works or who these people are either.

Which makes this a great time to introduce you to a couple of the cloud-builders.

Who Are Schrep and Jay?

There have been many thousands of contributors to Facebook's digital factory, including Zuckerberg's Harvard roommate, fellow computer science student and Facebook cofounder Dustin Moskovitz, who learned the necessary coding skills in a few days and jumped in to help Zuckerberg work through the technical challenges of expanding Facebook's infrastructure in the early days, and Jonathan Heiliger, a prolific networking expert and Facebook's vice president of infrastructure from 2007 to 2011. But no Facebook leaders have been cloud-builders longer than chief technology officer Mike Schroepfer and his vice president of engineering Jay Parikh.

Schroepfer, now in his early forties and affectionately known by all at Facebook as Schrep, arrived at Facebook in 2008 after stints as vice president of engineering at Mozilla—makers of Firefox, the number two Internet browser at the time—and Sun Microsystems after they acquired the datacenter provisioning company he had founded. With a bespectacled, what-you-see-is-what-you-get demeanor that is calm but projects competence and genuine enthusiasm for his and Facebook's work, Schrep—a master's in computer science from Stanford—is able to blend in completely with coders 20 years his junior at one of Facebook's overnight Hackathons that imagine and build prototypes for the future but can just as easily explain Facebook's complex technology on stage in front of an audience of hundreds of Facebook's multimillion-dollar advertising customers who know little about the technicalities but who want to know they are as safe with Schroepfer's teams' creations as they would be with television.

Parikh, who is now in his mid-forties and clearly still doesn't miss a workout, joined Facebook in 2009 after spending the majority of his previous career at Akamai, having started in the early days of the content delivery network responsible for 15–30% of the Internet's total traffic, a crucial background for the challenges that would lie ahead of him at Facebook. For someone who works in the boiler room of the Information Revolution with mind-numbingly large-scale speed and complexity and an unforgiving nature that usually thrusts you into the spotlight only if something has gone wrong, Parikh conveys a degree of energy and—more importantly—meaning that infects not just the others in the digital boiler room but thousands around him at Facebook and in the industry. For him, having to think about an entirely new generation of infrastructure when his teams are barely done building the current one is a feature of his job, not a bug.

Together, Schrep and Jay are responsible for every piece of hardware and software that plays a role in your happiness with Facebook's offerings:

(Network performance + Server performance) × Code efficiency =

But what is all this unseen, unheard, unmoving hardware and software?

Facebook's Wares: Hardware

Infra is the Latin prefix meaning "below" and also the internal shorthand at Facebook for the hardware infrastructure on which Facebook's software and services run and the teams that build and maintain it.

It is quite literally what lies below, right down to the land. In 2010 Facebook launched the first of what will be, by 2018, seven data centers owned and operated by the company around the world (in addition to the leased spaces in California and Virginia in which they operate):

▸ **Prineville, Oregon** (opened January 2010): 310,000 square feet

▸ **Forest City, North Carolina** (opened April 2012): 300,000 square feet

▸ **Luleå, Sweden** (opened June 2013): 300,000 square feet and a
planned future expansion

▸ **Altoona, Iowa** (opened November 2014): 300,000 square feet

▸ **Fort Worth, Texas** (opening 2016): up to 750,000 square feet over
time

▸ **Clonee, Ireland** (opening 2017): 300,000 square feet and a
planned future expansion

▸ **Los Lunas, New Mexico** (opening 2018): 510,000 square feet over
time

By the end of 2018, that will be about 50 football fields—more than half
the footprint of Disney's Magic Kingdom—worth of space for hardware
in buildings whose physical, mechanical and electrical configurations are
custom-designed by Facebook down to the open-air evaporative cooling
that avoids the energy inefficiency of air conditioning to reduce the heat
given off by the densely packed electrical equipment. Consequently, their
design has an industry-leading 1.07 power usage effectiveness (PUE) that
sees 92.5% of the power that arrives at the building making it to the hardware instead of being wasted in electrical transformers, converters or air
conditioning.

The sites—each of which cost more than $1 billion to build and re-
quires as much as 50 megawatts of electricity—are chosen for their low
cost and highly reliable and renewable energy (Sweden, Texas and New
Mexico will be 100% renewable, using hydro, wind and wind/solar power,
respectively), ample availability of water for evaporative cooling, rural location to reduce real estate cost and reasonable proximity to the Internet's
largest exchanges—on-ramps to the widest parts of the information su-
perhighway—and Facebook's users.

Once they've built the buildings, they need to connect to the Internet.
With some big pipes. While Facebook doesn't disclose their "egress"
speeds—the amount of data leaving all Facebook data centers in one second—we can extrapolate from comments and data in late 2015 that they
operate at many terabits per second.

Your high-definition stream of *Arrested Development* from Netflix is about 3 megabits per second, making Facebook's bandwidth millions of times that at your house.

Facebook's bandwidth needs are among its most rapidly growing, doubling in 2013 and astonishingly quintupling in 2014 with the adoption of video viewing in the News Feed. To give you some context, Table 7-2 shows Facebook's services as a percentage of all *mobile* Internet traffic around the world compared to their largest rival Google.

	North America	Europe	Middle East	Africa	Latin America	Asia Pacific
Facebook	**20%**	**16%**	**23%**	**15%**	**35%**	**10%**
Facebook	16%	16%	14%	5%	25%	8%
Instagram	4%		7%		3%	2%
Whats App			2%	10%	7%	
Google	**24%**	**24%**	**26%**	**9%**	**29%**	**20%**
Youtube	21%	21%	23%	5%	23%	18%
Other	3%	2%	3%	4%	6%	2%
Next Largest	**4%**	**2%**	**4%**	**7%**	**2%**	**3%**

Table 7-2. Percentage of mobile Internet traffic (Sandvine, Q4 2015)

Incredible bandwidth also needs to be maintained within the buildings as data travels to pods of many server racks, to individual racks within those pods and eventually to individual servers within those racks. This is known as switching, and for the sake of unadulterated speed dedicated to Facebook's network architecture, Facebook has architected all its own networking equipment.

Then, of course, come the servers themselves, where all those bits live and all the code to handle their relationships runs. You guessed it, Facebook also designed these themselves, stripping out everything they didn't need and building them so they can take server chips—each of which contains around a dozen CPUs—from either Intel or AMD to create flexibility and speed for upgrades.

Facebook doesn't disclose the number of servers it uses, but we can make some rough calculations based on the total power draw of their data centers, their power efficiency and the documented power envelopes of Facebook's server designs: It's possible that by the time its first six data centers are built out at the end of 2017 and filled with servers, Facebook could be running as many as a million servers with more than 30 million CPUs, making them one of the premiere cloud operators in the world, along with Google, Apple, Microsoft, Amazon and others who are also building out tens of millions of square feet of data centers around the world.

Facebook's Wares: Software

Once you have all that hardware, you need software to breathe life into it. Tens of millions of lines of code—and that's just the parts they've committed to the Open Source community where code is openly shared and improved upon across the industry.

Much of that software lives on Facebook's servers. On top of database technologies with unapproachable-sounding names like MySQL and memcache are services like the Facebook-built TAO (The Associations and Objects) that keeps track of trillions of things (e.g., people, things, comments) and relationships (e.g., Martin is friends with Steve, Steve checked in at Sydney's Opera House, Martin liked Steve's check-in) and that sees billions of requests *every second*, and the custom-built, aptly named Haystack, which stores and retrieves tens of billions of photos and videos.

It would be overwhelming for Haystack if it had to go all the way back to one particular server at one particular data center for each photo you want to see, so Facebook uses a software technique called "caching" to distribute popular pieces of data more widely throughout the Internet: the first time a piece of data—that picture of your friend's vacation—is requested and is not cached anywhere, it has to be retrieved from its originating server at a Facebook data center, but as it passes through the Internet back to you, it is cached first in an origin cache at the digital entrance of that data center, then at one of the thousands of edge caches all around the world at an Internet intersection close to you, and finally on your computer or phone. The next time you want to look at that picture, it's simply returned from your device. If a friend of yours in your Internet neighborhood wants to look at it, it's retrieved from the edge cache, and even someone from elsewhere around the world won't have to get it from the original backend server, as it will be returned to them from the origin cache at the entrance of the data center.

This works particularly well for Facebook for two reasons:

1. People want to retrieve something from Facebook (known as a "read," which caching can handle) 500 times as often as they want to deposit something (known as a "write," which has to make it all the way back to Facebook's one-source-of-truth database in the data centers).

2. Facebook's most popular pieces of data are *way* more popular than the rest: in a Facebook study of a random sample of 2.6 million viewed photos, 75% of users wanted to look at just 3.73% of the photos!
No wonder, then, that caching is crucial for Facebook and contributes significantly to your perceived performance of the service. Table 7-3 shows an example from sample photo data of how often a request can be taken care of at each layer of the cache network.

	Cache Success
Browser (your device)	65%
Edge (Internet intersection)	34.5%
Origin (data center)	14.5%
Backend (server)	9.9%

Table 7-3. Percentage of requests served by various Facebook caching levels

That's why caching is so valuable: With the original server only having to handle 9.9% of the requests, it is unloaded by a factor of 10, compared to not using caching.

But, it's not all about databases and servers. A significant amount of Schrep's teams' software resources also go to building and optimizing the experience we have on our phones, a challenge that's exploded in complexity over the years as the team has to address over 10,000 different kinds of phones—most of that due to the huge number of devices in the Google Android ecosystem—in a wide variety of network conditions around the world.

From its first mobile optimized website in 2007, to its first Apple iOS app in 2008 and Android app in 2009, to rewriting the iOS app in 2011 and completely rewriting it again in 2012 to double performance and significantly improve reliability, to launching the novel solution of Facebook Lite for emerging markets in 2015, the team is obsessed with every 100 milliseconds it can shave off when you start your Facebook app, when it has to access the network, process the resulting data, calculate the new screen layout of your News Feed, or send and receive messages; the team has built automated systems to mimic a broad range of devices and networks to automatically test every change they make.

All of this hardware and software can get a little esoteric, so let's take a look at a handful of specific projects that will feel a little more familiar to Facebook users.

Some of Facebook's Digital Factory's Greatest Technical Hits

485 million people in two years: Remember how at the end of 2009 Facebook was faced with growing more in a year than they had the first five and a half years? To accomplish the feat, they launched their first custom-designed data center, as well as their own high-performance optimization (HipHop for PHP and the HipHop Virtual Machine) of one of the Internet's most popular development languages, increasing the efficiency of their servers by over six times—the same effect as buying six times as many servers. Not only were they growing their hardware infrastructure size, they were making it radically more efficient at the same time.

The outcome of all that effort? The team was seamlessly able to support the addition of 485 million users in 2010 and 2011, the largest

24-month period of growth in Facebook's entire history—before or after. (see Figure 7.2).

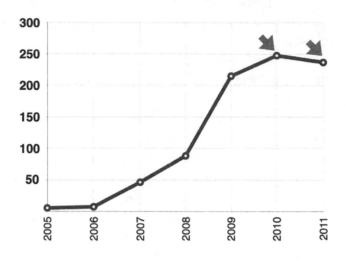

Figure 7-2. New Facebook monthly users (millions)

You would think that Facebook would guard all the technology that made this possible with the zeal Coke has for its original formula. Not so much. They gave it all away, contributing enabling software technologies like HipHop and HHVM to the Open Source software community and in April 2011 announcing the Open Compute Project (the brainchild of Heiliger) where, in a first for the hardware industry, they shared all the designs of their data center efforts—from servers to storage and networking and even building architecture—with the rest of the industry, including Apple, Microsoft and Google. These enabling technologies were important to Facebook but not as important as the larger technical community's ability to also embrace them and—more importantly—further advance their performance together.

In sharing these technologies for the greater good, Facebook joined the likes of Jonas Salk who did not patent his polio vaccine and Tesla, which open-sourced all their electric vehicle patents.

Instagration: Remember that massive change in Instagram's infrastructure back in 2013 when it had 200 million users and more than 20 billion photos? Me neither.

That's because the year-long project to migrate Instagram from its original infrastructure on Amazon's Web Services—infrastructure sold as a service to companies that don't have their own teams—to Facebook's infrastructure happened without a hitch.

It was a textbook example of an infrastructure team comprised of the Instagram team and their new Facebook colleagues going through a very complex process—they had to move the service through a *two*-step transition while it was *live*—with none of us on our phones any the wiser, in the process gaining scale, speed and reliability advantages to avoid site outages like the one that occurred to Instagram during an East Coast snowstorm in 2012. By December 2016, they had grown to more than 600 users and 40 billion photos (much more on the Instagram acquisition in Chapter 9).

Live video: We all know how Facebook revolutionized the way photos are shared and the huge storage and serving infrastructure that requires. Now imagine the impact on the size and complexity of that infrastructure when you add more than 8 billion video views per day and artificial intelligence to automatically analyze and compress different sections of uploaded videos with the encoding technique that will yield the highest quality and smallest size. Or the complexity of finding innovative ways to compress, store and deliver view-dependent adaptive bit rate streaming—say that three times fast—for much larger 360-degree videos in virtual reality.

According to Cisco, video is slated to become more than 80% of the Internet's traffic by 2019, and it's complicated to be sure. But perhaps none of it is as complicated as figuring out how to help Vin Diesel live-broadcast from his phone his thoughts about the latest movie scripts he's reading simultaneously to over a million of his nearly 100 million Facebook fans.

For a live broadcast, Facebook's systems no longer have the relative luxury of uploading a video, encoding that video carefully, storing it away and then retrieving it when someone wants to see it.

Instead, all of that has to happen in just two to three seconds, so that there doesn't appear to be a big lag between what Vin is talking about, his adoring fans seeing it and commenting on it, and for him to react back to them. Unfortunately, because Vin and so many other celebrities and public figures on Facebook are popular, their fans' enthusiasm for live broadcasts—which they can watch right in their Facebook News Feed—causes what the Facebook engineering team lovingly refers to as the "thundering herd" problem as people threaten to flood the live streaming server. So the team had to go back to its caching architecture and build a system that holds fans' requests to subscribe to the live stream at their local edge server, until the streaming server can push the video out to all those edge servers—each of which will handle about 200,000 simultaneous viewers—and ensure that each subsequent fan's request can be handled by the edge server, thus offloading the streaming server of about 98% of the requests it would have otherwise seen to make sure there's nothing standing in the way between Vin and his fans.

The Future of Facebook's Infrastructure: Sharks with Lasers

Around Facebook, Schroepfer and Parikh are fond of joking that their teams' ever expanding efforts know no boundaries, a notion that in its farcical extreme is best known as Dr. Evil's "sharks with frickin' laser beams" from the 1990s comedy, *Austin Powers: International Man of Mystery*.

The farther the teams go in pursuing Facebook's mission, however, the less farcical those lasers are becoming.

Connectivity: Having revolutionized the way *Facebook* connects to the Internet with their own data centers, network, servers and software, Facebook is now turning their attention to revolutionizing the way *people* connect to the Internet.

What's the only thing more complicated than building your own infrastructure here on earth? Building your own infrastructure in the sky.

We already heard in Chapter 5 about the AMOS-9 satellite that Facebook's coalition had planned to launch in 2016 to expand connectivity in sub-Saharan Africa, but Facebook is not stopping there. To cover less densely populated rural areas—not served cost-effectively by satellites—Facebook acquired British unmanned aerial vehicle (UAV, drones) maker Ascenta and is building solar-powered drones. With the wingspan of a 737. That weigh only about a third as much as a Toyota Prius. And use lasers to transmit data through the air to each other. At 10 gigabits per second. While in flight. At 60,000 to 90,000 feet. For three months at a time.

No, not sharks just yet, but damn good lasers accurate to the size of a dime over a distance of 11 miles while in flight.

A group of these drones, each covering a patch about 100 miles in diameter, will connect to a single terrestrial base station at a big Internet connectivity intersection using radio signals, relay the signal from drone to drone using lasers and then down to many smaller terrestrial base stations, which turn the radio signal into local WiFi or cellular connectivity for rural communities. The effort is intended to avoid expensive ground-based cable infrastructure and instead create new, more cost-effective modes of connectivity for operators or governments that don't have the means, or appetite, for these kinds of innovation risks themselves.

Drones, however, are not the only thing Facebook will do to work with network operators to discover new, more efficient approaches to connect the next few billion people (more in Chapter 14). In 2016, Facebook joined with the likes of AT&T, Verizon, Deutsche Telekom and SK Telecom on the Telecom Infra Project, which will extend the move-fast-and-share-things playbook of the Open Compute Project for data centers to the telecommunications infrastructure from access (the place where you connect to a network, such as a cellular tower or WiFi access point) to the core and the backhaul network in between.

Artificial intelligence: As advanced as drones are to communications infrastructure, so is artificial intelligence to software. The notion of teaching computers to learn—and think—will play an important role throughout Facebook's offerings in understanding photos, videos, speech and text, including its virtual assistant Facebook M (more in Chapter 13). As they have with much of their other software and hardware, Facebook is contributing their neural network training code and purpose-designed servers—artificial intelligence software learns better the more data it has to work with, making computing performance a fundamental limiter to progress—to the open source communities.

Virtual and augmented reality: And if all that reality wasn't enough, Facebook's *virtual* reality efforts—the Oculus VR acquisition (more in Chapter 15) also reports to Schrep—will deliver consumer hardware and a software ecosystem of experiences for our screens of tomorrow. Live 3D broadcast from Vin Diesel anyone?

Between the experiences on our phones, mind-boggling data center and telecommunications infrastructure innovations and future consumer interfaces, Facebook's digital factory has put its money and effort where its make-the-world-more-open-and-connect mouth is.

8

How Facebook Beat Google

LESSON 6:
Crossing the chasm is the best defense.

Background: Before you attack your competition—or are attacked by them—you have to understand each other's state of adoption among your customers and plan accordingly.

Facebook's Move: When Google came after them with a similar product, Facebook understood it had the advantage of having "crossed the chasm" with consumers. Instead of panicking, they doubled down on their strengths in the face of Google's attack.

Thought Starter: What is the state of adoption of your offering? What about that of your competitor(s)?

By the beginning of 2011, Facebook had vanquished the likes of Friendster, MySpace and Twitter, but comparatively those were the minor leagues of the Internet, and word was out that 800 pounds of Google were about to come after Facebook in earnest with a full-fledged social media offering called Google+ that would launch in the middle of 2011.

The natural instinct for describing a Google-vs.-Facebook conflict at that time would be to reach for the David and Goliath trope, but the reality was much darker for Facebook. Depending on your biblical interpretation, Goliath was between 6 feet 9 inches and 9 feet 9 inches and David about 5 feet 3 inches. Nothing like the actual difference between Google and Facebook, which was more like the difference between NBA center Shaquille O'Neal and a kitten.

At 24,400 employees, Google had nearly 12 times Facebook's 2,127.[1] (See Figure 8.1.)

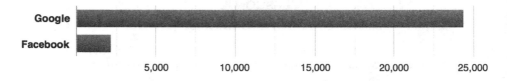

Figure 8-1. Employees (end of 2010)

On the business front, Google commanded 15 times Facebook's annual revenue at $29.3 billion vs. $1.974 billion and 14 times the net income at $8.5 billion vs. $606M.[2] Yes, Google's *profits* were four times greater than Facebook's *revenue*. (See Figure 8.2.)

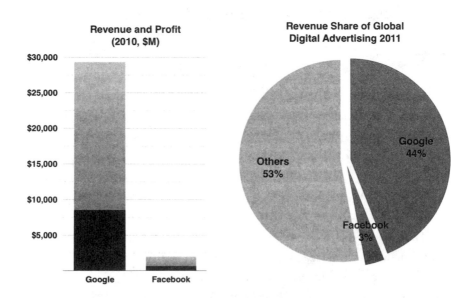

Figure 8-2. Revenue, profit and revenue share of global digital advertising

In 2011,[3] Google would not only have a monopolistic 85% share of search advertising but a 44% share of *all* digital advertising. Facebook's share? A minuscule 3.1%.

There was no way around it. As well as Facebook had done, this would be another level of competition entirely.

Everything at Stake for Facebook . . . Nothing for Google

Although coming into the head-to-head confrontation Google clearly outdistanced Facebook on business metrics, the two held more equal roles in the minds of people: Google as the leader in search (3.6 billion searches per day[4]) and Facebook the leader in social media (608 million monthly active users[5]).

The problem for Facebook was that if Google beat them at social media, there would be nothing left for them since Facebook at that time lacked other assets to fall back on.

Much less alarmingly for Google, if their incursion on Facebook failed, Google would simply remain the highly profitable Internet leader they already were.

These were the highest possible stakes for Facebook, and Google was *very* serious. It had begun in earnest in March 2010 when famed early Google employee and vice president of engineering Urs Hölzle penned a manifesto—dubbed the "Urs-quake" inside Google—pointing out the importance of the shift to social on the Internet and the need for Google to invest significant resources in making their products more people-centric. After campaigning heavily internally, Microsoft veteran and Google engineering leader Vic Gundotra was given the reins of the effort and moved to report directly to Larry Page, who had retaken the CEO role from Eric Schmidt in April 2011 and wasted no time in announcing to all employees that the company's success in social would affect 25% of everyone's bonus program.

Contrary to significant prior Google efforts that had grown organically with at most a few dozen employees, the Google+ effort would touch over a dozen products and more than two dozen teams comprising by some estimates as many as 1,000 people, many of whom worked in a building entirely dedicated to the effort.

Google had stumbled in prior efforts in the social space, whether in-house or through acquisitions or industry coalitions. Acquisition failures included their rejected offer to buy Friendster in 2003, not maneuvering photo service Picasa into a commanding position after the 2004 acquisition, never launching products based on acquisitions of the Dodgeball location service between 2005 and 2009, the Twitter-like Jaiku between 2007 and 2009, or the social Q&A service Aardvark in 2010 and not growing social app developer Slide after the 2010 acquisition. Failed in-house efforts included social media service Orkut, which launched in 2004 and grew to notable success only in Brazil, the confusing Wave from 2009 to 2010 and the troubled Gmail extension Buzz in 2010. As for industry coalitions, the OpenSocial API, designed to allow the portability of people's information between different social services, was never able to get Facebook on board and consequently withered.

None of that mattered now. Google+ was just the kind of focused, company-wide, everyone-rowing-in-one-direction effort Google needed to win.

And the pressure on Facebook was starting to show. In May 2011, Dan Lyons writing for Newsweek's *The Daily Beast*, exposed the fact that Facebook had secretly hired top global public relations firm Burson Marsteller—known especially for their crisis-management expertise—to prompt negative stories about Google's privacy practices in various media outlets including *USA Today*. The episode was an embarrassment for Burson Marsteller CEO Mark Penn, who had run Hillary Clinton's 2008 presidential campaign, as well as Facebook COO Sheryl Sandberg and her policy and PR chief Elliot Schrage, both of whom had worked for years to improve Facebook's perception of being trustworthy precisely on issues such as privacy.

Fixin' for a Fight

So, as summer 2011 neared, Google and Facebook prepared for their showdown.

Zuckerberg's handling of the circumstances is a good window into his general approach. He balanced a continued commitment to Facebook's mission and existing product plans with an elevated attention to focus and shipping products that was borne of a healthy paranoia—learned from leadership role model and former Intel CEO Andy Grove—about the increased competition Facebook would soon face. While he did call a "Lockdown"—60 days of redoubled focus that had its origin in tamping down competition at specific colleges in the early days of Facebook and was signified by a red neon sign above his conference room—and moved resources to key projects, there was no wholesale reshuffling of priorities or endless hand-wringing and dithering among Facebook's leadership team.

Democracies and consensus are not always optimal for nimbly and fearlessly responding—but not overreacting—to a threat. Zuckerberg's strong leadership (his strength of vision and historical success rate causes everyone at the company to gladly afford him a degree of paternalism that borders on being one of the most effective benevolent autocracies ever) prevented Facebook from losing the script in the face of very real danger.

Throughout the summer and early fall, Facebook would play defense in key areas of the Facebook experience in which they could be beaten by shipping high-res photos and a new photo viewer, an evolved Groups app, the integration of Skype for one-on-one video chat and a new version of profiles, dubbed "Timeline," combined with offense on new features, including the first iOS and Android versions of stand-alone Messenger, the first Facebook iPad app and the Follow function, which allowed you to subscribe to public updates from people—especially public figures—without having to become friends.

Google, in the meantime, was building a serious social media offering that—like Facebook—would have a user profile based on authentic identity, a "Stream" similar to Facebook's News Feed, a +1 function similar to Facebook's Like that was also integrated with Google Search to personalize your results and those of your friends, a Photos function integrated with Google's existing service Picasa and Pages to provide an opportunity for things like businesses to have a presence on the service similar to Facebook's own Pages. The two unique features of the service were Circles, a visual way to organize friends into groups in order to control who sees what content from you that was developed by no less a Silicon Valley eminence than original Macintosh system software programmer Andy Hertzfeld, and Hangouts for videoconferencing with up to ten people.

On June 28, 2011, Google+ stepped into the arena with a giant product, an equally giant PR blitz, and, after a twelve-week invite-only field trial, a giant blue arrow on their search page advertising Google+, a cross-promotional first for the company. Initial media coverage was positive, especially for Circles and their apparent advantages over Facebook's approach to managing who among your friends sees what.

Within two weeks of launch, Google+ grew to 10 million *registered* users—against the convention established by the likes of Facebook and Twitter, Google+ initially did not report *active* users—to 25 million in a month, to 40 million by October and to 90 million by the end of 2011.[6] All along, Facebook kept calmly shipping product while, like a duck fiercely paddling under the water, Sheryl Sandberg and her business teams kept a very close weekly eye on any Google+ numbers they could get their hands on and worked diligently to keep large business customers from becoming distracted with Google+ Pages and losing momentum on their respective Pages—and related advertising—on Facebook.

The year 2011 came to a close without much clarity on what exactly had happened between the two combatants. Neither had obviously won, but neither had obviously lost.

In February 2012, however, things became much clearer. Any potential perceived Google+ momentum came to a screeching halt when analytics firm comScore released a shocking finding: people were using Google+ only 3.3 minutes per person per month, while they were using Facebook for 7.5 hours. (See Figure 8.3.)

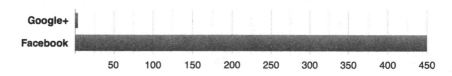

Figure 8-3. Minutes used per person per month

Google+ had not become a habit and had failed to pass its own CEO's "toothbrush test"—being used at least twice a day—which Page himself had reiterated as an expectation for Google's products on their July 2011 earnings call just after Google+'s launch.

Google+ would never recover. In June 2012, a year after launching and receiving maximum support and focus from the company and Page, Google+ had only 150 million monthly active users. In that same year, Facebook had not only *not* suffered any losses in its active user base, they had *grown* faster than Google+, adding about 200 million monthly active users, going from about 700 million when Google+ launched to about 900 million in the middle of 2012. Google+ would evolve in both function and face-saving public positioning into a mere "social layer" across Google's services like Gmail and YouTube, instead of an engaging destination like Facebook or Instagram. Its two don't-throw-the-baby-out-with-the-bathwater features—Hangouts and Photos—went on to become standalone applications.

By the time the dust of the heavily anticipated confrontation had settled, Facebook—the kitten to Google's Shaq—had stood in the ring and not only withstood Google's best shot but had defended its title and grown stronger.

How was that possible?

Lessons from 1962: Why Google+ Failed

During the development of Google+, the project's leaders commissioned a mural of a work by 19th-century German painter Albert Bierstadt for their building to remind the teams of the perils and potential of their project. Befitting the project's codename, "Emerald Sea," the painting depicted a rocky, frothy and wind-whipped ocean shore break with the conspicuously broken mast of a sailing ship being tossed about. Little did they know at the time that—just like the painting—their efforts would founder at the inhospitable shores of their competitor's unassailable asset.

Google had lost the Google+ battle with Facebook three years before it even launched.

That failure, it turns out, can be explained with research first made famous over 50 years ago by sociologist Everett Rogers and later extended by Silicon Valley author Geoffrey Moore. It was Rogers who in 1962 first published *Diffusion of Innovations*, the most extensive consolidation of over 500 studies across sociology, anthropology and geography into how innovations are communicated through certain channels and evaluated and adopted over time within social systems. It's important to realize that "innovation" in Rogers' context applies to circumstances as diverse as Paul Revere's April 18–19 1775 midnight ride (and the much less successful ride that night by William Dawes), the spread of kindergarten from Germany to the rest of the world between 1850 and 1910, the adoption of hybrid seed corn by farmers in Iowa in the 1930s, the first-businesspeople-then-consumers adoption of cellular telephones in Finland in the 1980s and 1990s, the Internet itself and the social networks of the 2010s.

A crucial distillation in Rogers' work is the identification of the different kinds of adopters along the timeline of innovations, as well as the surprisingly consistent size of each group as a fraction of the whole target population: 2.5% are Innovators, 13.5% Early Adopters, 34% the Early Majority, another 34% the Late Majority and 16% the Laggards.

It was marketer and consultant Geoffrey Moore who, in his 1992 *Crossing the Chasm*, expanded on that part of Rogers' work to identify the significant gap—the titular "chasm"—that exists in adoption behavior between the grouping of Innovators and Early Adopters (the first 16% of diffusion) and the grouping of the Early and Late Majority. He pointed out how difficult it can be to cross that chasm and the natural protection against later competitors (think of the chasm as a moat) that can result *if* you do.

Academic as that all may sound, it becomes very real when we take a look at Facebook and its diffusion among Internet users as a target population.

We can see in Figure 8-4 that, during 2009, Facebook crossed the proverbial chasm to exceed 16% diffusion and that by 2011 it had diffused through half of the early majority of Internet users globally (and had reached a total of 68% in the United States and more than 90% in countries like Mexico and Indonesia). Consequently, when Google launched Google+—a very similar product to Facebook's—in the summer of 2011, it did so into the teeth of a competitor who had already safely crossed into the heart of the consumer base and had on their side the switching costs, network effects and petabytes of learnings about 700 million consumers, who had spent up to seven years curating their authentic identity and connections on Facebook.

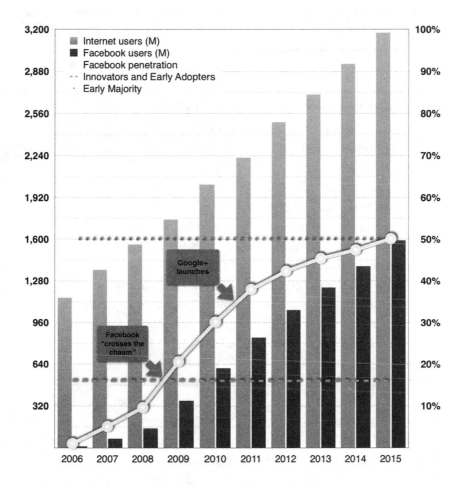

Figure 8-4. Facebook penetration among global Internet users

There are basically three kinds of players in consumer technology: (1) Those that are unable to cross the chasm in head-to-head competition (e.g., Twitter vs. Facebook), (2) those that innovate and are able to cross the chasm by relating their innovation to the Early Majority (e.g., Facebook in social, Google in search), and (3) those that try in vain to follow—and compete head-on with—existing chasm crossers. Google+ in its efforts against Facebook is the third kind.

For Google+ as it was conceived to have had a chance, it would have had to launch in 2008 while it could still compete with Facebook on the greener playing field ahead of the chasm with an audience of early adopters more open to a new thing.

Alternatively, in 2011, they would have needed to deliver a sufficiently differentiated product that reoriented the playing field enough to allow a newcomer to beat the incumbent the way Facebook beat MySpace or Instagram beat Twitter or Google's own search beat that of Yahoo. It's in this shift, however, that a technology company's greatest strength can become its greatest weakness:

> Google was technically and culturally the best in the world at getting you information and moving you onward across the Internet as fast as possible—to this day they proudly tell you just how fast they do so at the top of every search result—while Facebook had become the best at precisely the opposite: engaging you endlessly on their own properties in finding out what was happening in the lives of the people and things you were connected to.

Facebook's Magic Moment of seeing all your friends and their content—because you were where they were and vice versa—became Google+'s nightmare as shouts of "wasteland" and "ghost town" began to arise not long after the curiosity of its launch had worn off and people returned their attention to the comfortably worn and familiar confines of their Facebook News Feed. Even Google+'s most talked-about feature—Circles—was better in theory than in practice, as people didn't take the time to build and maintain Circles over time, proving that the burden of getting people the right information from the right people has to be shouldered by a superior algorithm from the network, not the handiwork of its users.

In the end, Google+ lost perhaps less to Facebook than to people's lack

of a perceived need to switch, a cautionary tale for all who think competing in the abstract world of digital must be easier than the hardscrabble
world of physical product.

Was there a way for Google to have competed more effectively in the
broader social space? Consumer technology may be one of the most difficult environments in which to answer backward-looking what-if questions, but with the luxury of hindsight one can't help but think that a
foray more inherently mobile, more focused on messaging and based on
an existing, much loved asset would have had greater success than
Google+.

That asset would have been Gmail, which at the time of Google+'s
launch had well over 200 million users, would grow to 425 million by the
middle of 2012 (when Google+ was faltering at 150 million) and eventually to 1 billion by February 2016.[7]

Gmail had a built-in map of connections between people (your e-mail
contact list), a frequency of use inherent to e-mail at the time (although
that's since been supplanted somewhat by instant messaging) and a natural fit with mobile. Somewhat tragically, this had occurred to Google who
in February 2010—more than a year before the launch of Google+—
launched Buzz, a Gmail extension that included social features such as
sharing links, photos, videos, status messages and commenting but that
failed spectacularly when upon launch it triggered a privacy furor as its
default settings exposed people's most e-mailed Gmail contacts publicly,
landing Google in a class-action lawsuit and an FTC settlement that
would require them to undergo annual privacy audits for 20 years and
caused the shuttering of Buzz around the time of the Google+ launch.
The Buzz failure—at the worst possible time—essentially destroyed
Google's last best hope for head-to-head competition with Facebook in
social.

Apex Predators:
The Future of Google and Facebook

The case of Google+'s failure is a window into the rivalry between Google
and Facebook. Facebook won that round and in the five years since has
become a business of consequence in a similar class as Google's, leading

to the establishment of two suns—and their respective solar systems—largely in control of the Internet.

The two—separated by only four exits on the main Silicon Valley traffic artery US 101—have carved out big leadership positions on opposite sides of the $168 billion 2016 global digital advertising chessboard,[8] the fastest growing part of the advertising industry and the part expected to overtake television for largest total spend, starting in the United States in 2016:

> ▸ **Google led in search advertising**: 72% share of $29 billion in the United States alone

> ▸ **Facebook led in display advertising**: 29.3% share of $32 billion in the United States alone, with Google at just 15.7% (and Facebook especially strong in the native and mobile formats that will lead the way in the future)

While Google's share of the total digital advertising pie was still a leading—but declining—40% in 2016, Facebook had more than quadrupled their share since 2010 to become the definitive number two at 13.2% and growing.

All of which has led to an uneasy detente.

Google and Facebook are the apex predators in their respective spaces and together are projected to account for a dominant 73% of all additional digital ad spending between 2016 and 2018.[9] However, the two have failed to invade each other's core businesses. Facebook's effort at search—awkwardly called Graph Search—failed to make a dent in Google's search business similar to the failure of Google+ in social. In classic Silicon Valley co-opetition, the two even depend on each other. Facebook depends on Google for access to Android-based smartphones, which are the vast majority of the devices dominating the foreseeable future and the apps for which—including Facebook, WhatsApp, Messenger and Instagram—are controlled by the terms and conditions of the Google-owned Play Store. Google, in turn, depends on Facebook—the most important lens on your digital world—for referral traffic, especially to YouTube.

The cautious mutual eyeing is sure to continue. As far as future competition is concerned, over the long term it will be easier for Facebook to invade Google's turf—beyond brand loyalty, search lacks consumer lock-in or network effects and is powered by relatively commoditized algorithms and merely needs a search box and lots of visitors—than for Google to invade Facebook's, especially now that the latter has large assets across social media *and* messaging. While Google may be the very lucrative winner of the past and present, Facebook is its very interesting future.

9

How Facebook Became More Than Facebook

LESSON 7:

Disrupt yourself before someone else does.

Background: Disruption is inevitable and, in the modern connected economy, can come more swiftly than ever. To retain the initiative—especially when you're winning—shape that disruption through your own moves instead of falling victim to those of others.

Facebook's Move: Zuckerberg began a string of self-disruption when he struck swiftly in a one-on-one engagement with the CEO to acquire Instagram before a large competitor did or a smaller competitor grew to make things uncomfortable. The successful integration of Instagram proved that Facebook was the place to be for the world's best builders, enabling an ongoing diversification through a multi-app strategy.

Thought Starter: How would you disrupt yourself? Do it now.

In early 2012, eight years into Facebook's journey, the then 27-year-old Mark Zuckerberg had every excuse in the world to be complacent.

Facebook had over 900 million monthly users around the world, making it the largest property on the web and mobile and the unquestioned champion of where people spent their time online every day. One-time threats including MySpace, Twitter and Google+ were comfortably in Zuckerberg's rearview mirror and fading.

Facebook was a profitable business, with $3.7 billion of revenue the prior year and in the middle of the so-called "quiet period" mandated by the U.S. Securities Exchange Commission between filing its S-1 registration and prospectus and holding its highly anticipated initial public offering in May at a stock price that would value it in excess of $100 billion.

You would have had to work hard to come up with ways to make things go better.

But Zuckerberg is a student. Of the classics. Of Hannibal. Of chess (in 2014 he would ask world champion Magnus Carlsen for a lesson and elicit an "incredibly quick learner" review from the master). Of business. Including lessons he received personally about paranoia from Andy Grove, focus from Jeff Bezos and the long view from Bill Gates.

Complacency isn't his thing.

In early 2012, Zuckerberg was thinking farther ahead about Facebook's mission than nearly anyone realized. And it started with a fledgling photo-sharing app that had a mere 10 million users in the fall of 2011.

Understanding Kevin Systrom and Instagram

We may give technology leaders too much credit when we mythologize them—Steve Jobs certainly would not have been able to get Apple off the ground without Steve Wozniak—but, just as dogs tend to look like their owners, so too Silicon Valley companies tend to be most heavily influenced by their founder CEOs.

Mike Krieger, Instagram's second employee, plays a crucial Wozniak-like role in the company, but to understand Instagram is to understand its CEO, Kevin Systrom.

Systrom, just five months older than Zuckerberg, grew up on the East Coast and went to Middlesex School, a boarding school in Massachusetts and an hour's drive from Zuckerberg's high school alma mater Phillips Exeter Academy in New Hampshire. While at Middlesex, Systrom—foreshadowing his future—continued to develop his interest in computer programming and served as president of the photography club.

Formalizing his hobbies, he graduated from Stanford with a degree in management science and engineering while also diving deeper into photography during a term abroad where, according to a *Vanity Fair* profile, instructors encouraged him to use Holga plastic lens cameras, which take square photos on traditional film—as well as complex chemical combinations in developing the film.

At Stanford, Systrom also had his first intersection in 2004 with fellow East Coast transplants Zuckerberg and Facebook cofounder Adam d'Angelo, who tried to hire him to a very nascent Facebook. He passed on that initial offer but continued to cross paths with the two in years to come.

During an internship at Silicon Valley podcasting company Odeo, which would pivot to become the much more well-known Twitter, he sat at the desk next to cofounder and eventual CEO Jack Dorsey, whom we will meet again in this story.

Two years at Google, one on products like Gmail and one on corporate business development, rounded out his Silicon Valley apprenticeship.

Beyond all the technology, however, deep down style matters to Systrom.

▸ **Style in the form of fashion**: His own and the entirety of the fashion industry. In a move completely opposite to Zuckerberg's one-note gray-T-shirt-and-jeans wardrobe, Systrom has replaced the ties and khakis of his Middlesex years with Brioni suits, Charvet knit ties and Lanvin sneakers. He doesn't just appreciate the style of designers like Diane von Fürstenberg, Karl Lagerfeld and Donatella Versace, tastemakers like editor Anna Wintour, model Gigi Hadid, chef Jamie Oliver and photographer Annie Leibovitz and celebrities like Kim Kardashian West, actor Russell Brand, athlete Boris Becker, actress Lena Dunham and musician Harry Styles. He has pictures of himself together with them in his Instagram feed. While Zuckerberg held his wedding in his own backyard, Systrom and wife Nicole held their reception at a nightclub and speakeasy built for them at exclusive Napa Valley winery Clos Pegase.

▸ **Style in the form of music**: As a teen in Boston, Systrom worked at a record store where, according to a feature in *Vegas Seven*, he sold records to famous DJs, including Paul Oakenfold, Tiesto and Paul van Dyk. In college he moonlighted as a DJ and more recently was featured behind the turntables—as DJ Systromatic—at Las Vegas nightclub Rain, where he was joined by actor Adrian Grenier of HBO's *Entourage*, Prince Fahad of Saudi Arabia and EDM group Far East Movement.

▸ **And style in the form of photography**: Not only does Systrom have a deep appreciation for great photography, he proves a capable lensman in the hundreds of pictures he posts in his own Instagram feed @kevin.

It's no wonder that style came to play a crucial role in Instagram's story, which doesn't actually start with Instagram.

Instead, it started in early 2010 as Burbn, a feature-laden, location-oriented social network built by Systrom and Krieger. By July, however, Burbn was facing dire issues with growth—according to Krieger, usage topped out at about 1,000 people—and competition including Foursquare, SCVNGR and Facebook's imminent launch of location-oriented features called Places.

Remember that Odeo-to-Twitter pivot? Systrom and Krieger were wise enough to realize that Burbn needed a similar reboot.

Krieger himself has said that "working on a startup is a balancing act: being crazy enough to believe your idea can take off, but not crazy enough to miss the signs when it's clearly not going to." Burbn fell into the latter category, so the two worked throughout the summer to reduce the app to the essence of the few features users *did* care about and designed an obsessively focused—and, yes, stylish—social photo sharing-and-discovery app aimed at letting you share life's moments. Without Systrom's authentic passion for photography and style, this radical honing would have been hard to imagine.

On October 6, 2010, the newly christened Instagram launched. It featured simple ways to:

▸ Take a square picture (remember Systrom's Holga camera?).

▸ Apply one of 11 filters that digitally recreated darkroom manipulations (remember Systrom's chemicals?) that gave your picture a sense of sophistication beyond what you would attach to a text message.

▸ Connect with others to share your photos.

▸ Discover and "like" photos from others in a nothing-but-photos scrolling feed that echoed the importance of a feed to Facebook and also differentiated Instagram from other popular photo apps at the time, including Hipstamatic, which had launched in 2009, featured filters, had millions of users and would win Apple's iOS Photo App of the Year 2010 award but had no sharing or discovery.

▸ Share photos to other platforms including Facebook, Twitter, Tumblr and Flickr.

It was a stylish visual experience that invited users to reciprocate, creating an implicit expectation among its community that you curated what you shared. Every carefully constructed photo you saw reinforced that you should carefully construct the next photo you shared.

To this day, that is the unique difference of the Instagram community, 600 million strong by December 2016 and using an app that at its core has remained largely unchanged in five years. While you are primarily on Facebook because of *whom* you are connected to, you are on Instagram because of *what* you see.

Behind the scenes, Krieger had made the two hardest parts feel fast— uploading pictures to Instagram and scrolling the photo-heavy feed smoothly on iPhones that had a fraction of the performance we're used to today. This kind of "boiler room" work is often overlooked by outsiders but is crucial to mobile usage and the app's success.

Instagram was the very model of the mobile-only "minimally viable product" that is fetishized in Silicon Valley: simple for people to grasp, use and become addicted to.

Within 24 hours of launch, it had grown to 25,000 users. Three months later, it had one million users. And a year after its launch, 10 million.

Playing a Much Bigger Game

Although Instagram had caught the attention of the Silicon Valley elite—an A-list of investors including former Facebooker d'Angelo, Twitter's Dorsey, angel investor Chris Sacca and top-tier institutional investors Benchmark Capital, Andreessen Horowitz, Baseline Ventures and Greylock Partners had put money into the company in two rounds of financing—and the app had been runner-up Best Mobile App at the TechCrunch awards in early 2011; by late 2011, it had just one-tenth the monthly users of Twitter and roughly one-hundredth those of Facebook.

Zuckerberg, however, was watching more closely than most and had an ace up his sleeve when it came to data. Because Instagram was using Facebook's Connect platform to enable sharing—and Facebook being by far the largest platform Instagram was using for that purpose—Zuckerberg had nearly real-time awareness of Instagram's relative growth and engagement, rather than the occasional glimpse into the growth of the app the unwashed masses would get when Instagram deigned to share that information. Few people in the industry had more familiarity with looking at this kind of growth data with their teams than Zuckerberg, and unlike the stock market, historical performance of these apps do tell clear stories—or at least strongly inform hunches—about their futures.

It lined up perfectly because not only could he presage Instagram's future better than practically anyone, bringing Instagram into the Facebook fold fit the model of something much, much bigger he had been thinking about: The dawn of Facebook-the-mission no longer just equaling Facebook-the-app—what would come to be known as the multi-app strategy internally and the family of Facebook apps and services externally.

Systrom had built an app as true to what mattered most to him as Facebook was to what mattered to Zuckerberg. The two could not only coexist but benefit from being under the same roof of the mission to make the world more open and connected. Zuckerberg was prescient—and perhaps egoless—enough to know that Facebook's app was not the only way that people would want to share—especially in the crucial medium of photos—and Instagram was the perfect first step to protecting Facebook's mission and bringing together a set of complementary apps.

Instagram would not just be a nice adjacent use-case to Facebook. A second unusually high-engagement property with opportunities for expanded advertising revenue over time. A great audience (although more than 90% of Instagram's users are also on Facebook, Instagram skews to the appealing millennial demographic with nearly 75% of users under the age of 35, making Instagram the second youngest skewing audience of the largest global social media platforms after Snapchat; on Facebook, more than 50% of users are over 35). A different kind of feed from Facebook that does not require the use of an authentic identity and has no algorithm choosing the best content for you. Or even just another weapon to combat Twitter and Snapchat and crucially win the hearts and minds of celebrities and public figures who were making those platforms their home and drawing their fans with them.

It would be the first domino to fall in a sequence that would lead to a stunning four out of the top five most used social apps in the world belonging to Facebook.

Before all of that could happen, however, Zuckerberg would need to acquire Instagram, the details of which are another window into how he operates as Facebook's captain.

The New York Times would report in December 2012 that Twitter—led by early Instagram investor and old Systrom desk neighbor Jack Dorsey—had actually made a pass at an Instagram acquisition in March of 2012 at a valuation of $525 million, although whether this offer was formally extended is a matter of contention. At around the same time, Silicon Valley venture capital heavyweight Sequoia Capital made an offer to Instagram to lead a new round of investment (along with Greylock Partners, Benchmark Capital and Thrive Capital) that would bring a $50 million infusion at a $500 million valuation.

Systrom (recall his experience in Google's corporate business development group) and Krieger determined at that point that they would take the new round of investment, which closed on Wednesday April 4 and, according to a feature in *Vanity Fair*, informed both Twitter CEO Dick Costolo—who is said to have been less passionate about an Instagram acquisition than Dorsey—and Zuckerberg of the news that day.

Strikingly definitively and unilaterally, Zuckerberg invited Systrom to his house that Friday and offered a $1 billion acquisition that would practically overnight double the value of Instagram, which at the time was a mere 14 months old, had 30 million monthly users, 13 employees and exactly $0 in revenue.

The two negotiated the deal essentially among themselves—with a few key details courtesy of Facebook's prolific director of corporate development Amin Zoufonoun—in 48 hours. On Sunday, Zuckerberg informed the Facebook board of the acquisition—his controlling interest in Facebook makes the board's approval a mere formality—and it was announced publicly on Monday, April 9.

While Zuckerberg had completed end-to-end acquisition conversations over a single weekend before—the $47.5 million FriendFeed acquisition in 2009, which had brought CTO-to-be Bret Taylor to Facebook—the size and speed of the Instagram acquisition and its timing in the middle of an IPO quiet period were unprecedented and possible only because of the way Zuckerberg had structured Facebook and the mixture of paranoia and strategy—and in Silicon Valley you treat those two impostors the same— he employed to lead, using that corporate structure when the situation called for it.

Although at the time, a $1 billion price tag for Instagram was considered lofty, it would turn out to be the ultimate Moneyball acquisition for Zuckerberg—a superior investment because Zuckerberg had better data and a better strategy than anyone else. That it was also good defense against a possible acquisition of Instagram by Twitter was a mere bonus.

Two and a half years after the acquisition announcement, Instagram would grow to more monthly users than Twitter and present a significant advantage in time spent per person and daily engagement. By September 2015, it had gone on to reach 400 million monthly users, while Twitter had to confess in its Q4 2015 earnings report that it had for the first time in its history declined quarter-over-quarter in monthly users to 305 million. As of June 2016, Instagram stood at 500 million users, and would grow to 600 million a mere six months later (see Figure 9.1).

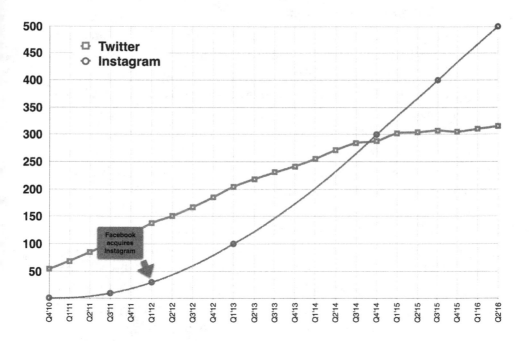

Figure 9-1. Twitter vs. Instagram global monthly users (millions)

To add insult to injury, at the beginning of 2016, Instagram had started to win the war over engagement with so-called public content—especially celebrities—with folks like footballer Cristiano Ronaldo at 49 million Instagram followers (only 40 million on Twitter), Beyoncé at 61 million (only 14 million on Twitter) and singer Taylor Swift getting nearly 20 times as many likes for photos such as her 2016 Grammy win on Instagram than on Twitter, even though she has 72 million followers on Twitter compared to 68 million followers on Instagram.

Slowly and very deliberately—keep in mind the importance of the Instagram community's sensibilities and style consciousness—the teams began to integrate advertising into the Instagram experience, relying deeply on their experience growing advertising on Facebook and the powerful infrastructure to target, deliver and measure advertising that Sheryl Sandberg and the team had already built.

It began with an announcement to the community of the coming arrival of ads on Instagram in October 2013 and a period during which

Systrom himself approved the earliest ads that were delivered in collaboration with only a few large brands to ensure focus on quality creative and a thoughtful approach to the audience that brands like Michael Kors, Burberry and Mercedes—who were already active members of the Instagram community—were keen on in order to preserve long-term brand opinion.

Given the quality of the overall environment—think placing your ad inside the editorial quality of a magazine like *Vogue*—and the desirability of the younger, highly engaged audience, the proposition was like catnip to premium advertisers, the perfect first wave of commercial participants in Instagram's community.

In September 2015, after two years of careful testing—for a man on a mission, Zuckerberg has tremendous patience when the situation calls for it—Facebook announced the expansion of the availability of Instagram photo, video, carousel and Shop Now ads from a few hundred brand advertisers to all businesses using the Facebook advertising tools in 30 countries around the world. Instagram had become an option in Facebook's advertising engine, including the interfaces into that engine that large advertising agencies could plug into on behalf of their clients and the all-important "self-serve" tools that made Facebook's advertising platform directly accessible to people and businesses of any size.

Plugging into that infrastructure, and—because over 90% of Instagram users overlapped between Facebook and Instagram and could be matched across the two services—bringing Facebook's understanding of people to Instagram delivered all of Facebook's proven power of buying, targeting and measuring advertising to Instagram, including the ability to run advertising on both services at the same time.

To drive home the power of living inside Facebook's ad engine, by February 2016—just six months after opening ads to all businesses—Instagram had gone from hundreds of monthly advertisers to 200,000 (and would reach 500,000 by September 2016), far more than the 130,000 active advertisers Twitter amassed in the first five years of its ad offering and still only a fraction of the over 4 million advertisers on Facebook for whom Instagram advertising is but a check box away.

With impression-based pricing holding constant above Facebook levels, even while many new advertisers came to Instagram, user engagement with ads exceeding even that of Facebook and advertising outcomes like recall exceeding norms across the industry by nearly three times, as measured by advertising arbiter-of-choice Nielsen, the years of testing were paying off. Literally: while Facebook does not break out Instagram advertising revenue in its reporting, Zuckerberg made it clear within the company that he expected Instagram to catch and exceed Twitter's revenues—$2.2 billion in 2015—quickly, and with analysts Credit Suisse estimating Instagram revenue could be around $3 billion in 2016, the team appeared well on its way to meeting Zuckerberg's wishes.

Three years after the announcement of the acquisition, Instagram had become—in addition to all its other benefits—a powerful new S-curve of revenue for Facebook.

Making the Future More Possible

But even that is not the Instagram acquisition's greatest gift.

To understand how that can be, let's go back to that April weekend in 2012 when Systrom and Krieger agreed to be acquired. Why did they choose Facebook over both Twitter and staying independent?

Prior to the Instagram acquisition, Facebook had done more than 20 acquisitions, on each occasion either shutting down the company's products or integrating them into the larger Facebook offerings. In the case of Instagram, however, Zuckerberg painted a vision of enabling the growth and success of a separate product with the support of some of the world's best infrastructure, growth, product and advertising teams and technologies while retaining significant autonomy to build the service Instagram was dreaming of. It was a founder-friendly win–win vision that appealed to the kind of builder more focused on all the capabilities necessary to become a truly impactful business than whether or not they rang the bell at the NASDAQ the day of their IPO. It didn't hurt that Zuckerberg had cultivated a relationship with the like-minded Systrom over the course of eight years, a crucial but little understood difference-maker on many occasions for Zuckerberg, who is mostly abbreviated by the media as socially awkward.

The skeptical observer will wonder how Systrom could know that Zuckerberg's vision would actually come to pass.

And therein lies the priceless value of the Instagram story: proof of existence that Zuckerberg can turn visions of growth and impact into reality without undue meddling. A clear message to the best builders in the world that if you want to play truly big, come work with Facebook.

In February 2014, with Instagram already approaching 200 million users, this would play a big role in Jan Koum's global messaging phenom WhatsApp agreeing to join Facebook in a blockbuster $22 billion acquisition (it has since gone from 400 million monthly users to over a billion by early 2016).

A month later, it played a role in upstart virtual reality headset maker Oculus VR believing that being a part of Facebook in a $2 billion acquisition was its best way forward.

Three months after that, it played a role in Zuckerberg's ability to recruit highly respected PayPal CEO David Marcus to Facebook to oversee its Messenger platform working for Zuckerberg (it has since become Facebook's *3rd* service with over a billion monthly users, a milestone it reached in July 2016).

And it's not a stretch to suggest that it has played a role in everything from the acquisition of UK high-altitude unmanned aerial vehicle maker Ascenta, which is a part of Facebook's Connectivity Lab enabling Zuckerberg's vision of connecting the next few billion people around the world, to artificial intelligence pioneer Yann LeCun joining Facebook to build its artificial intelligence lab, a crucial building block in all of Facebook's services being more able to understand, reason, plan and remember content and people.

Perhaps the only significant time it did *not* play a role was in Facebook's failed attempt to acquire messaging and discovery app Snapchat, which was estimated at over 200 million monthly users in the middle of 2015 with as many as 70% under the age of 25, according to CivicScience. Zuckerberg first made an overture to Snapchat CEO Evan Spiegel in December 2012, reportedly offering $1 billion to acquire the service. Spiegel declined, and in the fall of 2013—on the eve of Facebook launching its direct competitor to Snapchat called Poke, which would fail to get traction—Zuckerberg came calling again, this time reportedly offering $3 billion. Spiegel declined again, ironically echoing Zuckerberg's own decision to pass on Yahoo's $1 billion acquisition offer, and later appeared to starkly contrast acquisition with growth when he suggested in *Forbes*,

"There are few people in the world who get to build a business like this. I think trading that for some short-term gain isn't very interesting." Snapchat has since gone on to subsequent private funding events reportedly valuing it in excess of $16 billion, and in October 2016 *The Wall Street Journal* projected Snap Inc., Snapchat's parent company, may go public at a valuation in excess of $25 billion as early as March 2017.

In the beginning, creating a company was the best way to bring people together toward Facebook's mission. The Instagram acquisition—and more importantly its postacquisition success—have turbo-boosted that principal, and every subsequent acquisition that it made more possible has reinforced it.

It has created an ever-growing gravity for the single most important thing Zuckerberg needs for the success of Facebook in the long term: the desire of the world's best people and their creations to join with him.

10

How Facebook Plays the Long Game

LESSON 8:
Some long games are worth playing if you take care of business in the meantime.

Background: Facebook has been very successful helping people connect—and building related advertising revenue—in many places around the world. Most notably lagging behind those successes are China (Facebook's services are blocked, and competition is stiff), Japan (competition has kept Facebook from taking a greater share of the lucrative advertising market) and India (only 30% of the population is on the Internet).

Facebook's Move: Zuckerberg has accepted that overcoming the inherent challenges in China, Japan and India will take time. He is able to pursue these worthwhile but uncertain long games because more essential elements of the business are doing well.

Thought Starter: Are you playing a long game? Is it worth it? How are you thriving in the meantime?

One Step Forward in Cairo,
Two Steps Back in Beijing

It's not hard to imagine the furrowed brows in Beijing in early 2011 as nearly 4,700 miles to the West events were unfolding in Cairo.

Fomented by dissatisfaction with political, economic and human rights conditions, brought to the fore mostly by the younger generation, North Africa and the Middle East experienced a series of internal civil upheavals starting in late 2010. The Arab Spring began in Tunisia, quickly spread to Algeria and Jordan, and then—most publicly—to Egypt where the 30-year reign of Hosni Mubarak came under siege during 18 days of country-wide protests, including as many as 250,000 people in Cairo's Tahrir Square, that would eventually see the autocrat resign in February 2011, with power transferring to Egypt's Armed Forces, the parliament being dissolved and the 30-year "emergency law" and national constitution suspended.

Of Egyptians polled after the events, 85% credited social media—particularly Facebook and Twitter—with raising awareness inside the country on the cause of the movements, spreading information to the world about the movement, organizing actions and managing activists.[1] Of those surveyed, 95% indicated they used Facebook to get news/information during the civil movements, as opposed to 86% using local, independent or private media and just 48% using regional or international media. Appropriately deflecting credit, Facebook's leadership would point out that theirs was merely a tool and that change was being brought about not by the platform but by people, one of whom—ironically—was former Google employee Wael Ghonim, who played a leading role in calling for protests in Egypt and was one of the administrators of a Facebook Page titled "We Are All Khaled Saeed" (in memoriam of an Egyptian citizen who had been arrested and later died in custody as a consequence of police brutality in mid-2010), which had hundreds of thousands of followers.

Nevertheless, the connection between social media and large-scale political upheaval with profound consequences had been made to a greater extent than ever before, and by February 2012 rulers had been forced out in Tunisia, Egypt, Libya and Yemen, uprisings were reaching rarely seen levels in Bahrain and Syria and protests were occurring in Algeria, Iraq, Jordan, Kuwait, Morocco and Sudan.

Beijing was paying attention. The ability of the Middle East populace—especially the younger contingent—to rise up and throw off its leadership with the help of social platforms, while a "win" for places like Egypt (although the long arc of history continues to be complicated as Mohamed Morsi, democratically elected in June 2012, would be overthrown by the Egyptian military just a year later in July 2013), was a new wave of proof of the most visceral kind that China's restrictive Internet policies—known in the West as the Great Firewall, which blocks services like Facebook—were precisely appropriate for the goals of the country's communist government. Whether fundamental instigator or mere organizational tool, these services were not just abstractly incendiary.

Seeing its Middle East ally Mubarak deposed via internal civil pressure—instead of the traditional seen or unseen external political pressure from places like America—was striking, and China took substantial action to avoid "political contagion" between the Middle East and its own population by censoring terms like "Egypt" and "Jasmine" (a flower symbolizing solidarity with Tunisia's Jasmine Revolution) in Internet searches, disallowing the sale of Jasmine flowers, suppressing the efforts of foreign journalists reporting on possible effects of revolutions in the Middle East and detaining human rights advocates including artist Ai Weiwei.

In light of this weighty history and Facebook's stated mission of making the world more open and connected—arguably the precise opposite of a government intent on controlling information both internally and across borders—success for Zuckerberg in China will be a long and uncertain game, and it is only one of three such efforts in which the Menlo Park company is engaged.

Facebook's Big Long Game: China

At stake in China for Facebook are the twin pillars of user growth and revenue. Even a 30% penetration—half that of the United States and less than a third that of the Philippines—of the country's 674 million Internet users would make China Facebook's largest country by users. And

China's total advertising market is projected to be $67 billion in 2018,[2] making a share of the business even just half that of Facebook's in the United States—about 4.4% in 2015 on $8.3 billion out of $187 billion[3]— worth $1.5 billion annually with an upside to $2.5 billion when taking into consideration that digital advertising is projected to be nearly 50% of all advertising in China as opposed to the 28% it is projected to be in the United States. At the revenue multiples Facebook was being afforded on Wall Street in the middle of 2016, that could add up to as much as a $40 billion increase in valuation, the same as Twitter, Snapchat and Pinterest *combined.*

Standing in Facebook's way are the interconnected forces of censorship and local competition. Blocking has been in place consistently since 2009 for Facebook, Instagram and Messenger (and off-and-on for WhatsApp), while local services—operating under tight rules for user identity, censorship and encryption—are thriving.

While the Chinese constitution affords freedom of speech and press, it allows authorities to crack down on "producing, posting or disseminating pernicious information that may jeopardize state security and disrupt social stability, contravene laws and regulations and spread superstition and obscenity."[4] According to the Council on Foreign Relations, to effect these crackdowns, China's Golden Shield Project—the actual name of the Great Firewall—has been running since 1998 and engages in bandwidth throttling, keyword filtering (especially around forming collective action, ethnic strife, official corruption, police brutality, the Tiananmen Square protests of 1989, freedom of speech, democracy and blocking access) and techniques as basic as shuttering the sites of certain publications, as sophisticated as deep packet inspection and as totalitarian as shutting down the entire Internet as they did for 10 months in 2009 following ethnic riots in the far western Xinjiang province deemed to have been enabled by the Internet. Beyond the digital effort, the government also engages in deterrents like jailing dissident journalists, bloggers and activists; dismissals; demotions; libel lawsuits; fines and forced TV confessions.

To operate in China, services have to carefully balance the country's mandate to store data on Chinese users in China (where the government has the right to access it whenever they want, as is already the case for American companies such as Apple, Uber and LinkedIn), while assuring existing users outside of China that their data will not leak to the Chinese government and submitting to strict censorship guidelines that are refreshed weekly by the Communist Party Central Propaganda Department and Bureau of Internet Affairs, enforced by more than 100,000 people in state and private employ[5] and observed by another 2 million people employed as "opinion analysts" who report on—but do not censor—Internet goings-on.[6]

Whether you consider these measures draconian or not (France-based watchdog group Reporters Without Borders ranked China 175th out of 180 countries in its 2014 index of press freedom), they are the way of a land carefully managing an information pressure valve between a sense of total oppression on one extreme (think North Korea) and power-altering overthrow on the other (think Tahrir Square). Zuckerberg has made it clear that Facebook—in contrast to Google, which rejected China's censorship in the early days, subsequently shuttered its China operations and is now slowly crawling back—intends to respect and operate within the system on the way to finding success.

Perhaps more problematic even than censorship, Facebook faces daunting competition—or, for the more cynical, a cocktail of economic protectionism—in building something Chinese users would embrace in addition to wildly popular local products like the messenger WeChat (called Weixin in China where it has more than 600 million users), the micro blogging service Weibo (similar to Twitter, with over 250 million users[7]) and social network RenRen (most like Facebook, with over 200 million users[8]), which offer sophisticated takes in connecting people and enabling entertainment and commerce.

Zuckerberg, Sandberg, communications and policy leader Elliott Schrage, veteran corporate and business development vice president Vaughan Smith and Asia Pacific vice president Dan Neary, who has two decades of experience in the region, are well aware of the patience with which they will need to operate to understand China's politics, economy and people and to deliver a product and business model that fits within that understanding but still exerts some advantage over the dominant incumbents embraced by both the government and hundreds of millions of users.

Zuckerberg has made a point of personal meetings with Xi Jinping,

China's president and general secretary of the Communist Party (said to hold the most consolidated degree of power over China since Mao Zedong), propaganda chief and member of the Communist Party's Politburo Committee Liu Yunshan, Internet czar Lu Wei and Jack Ma, China's biggest homegrown entrepreneur and CEO of commerce giant Alibaba. The American's ability to speak Mandarin, his lectures at Tsinghua University, giving of a Chinese name to daughter Max (Mingyu roughly translates to "bright universe") and marriage to Priscilla Chan—whose parents are Chinese-Vietnamese refugees who immigrated to the United States—even led state-run television broadcaster China Central Television to dub Zuckerberg "a son-in-law of China." Sandberg, who as a Disney board member, has had a front-row seat for part of CEO Bob Iger's 18-year journey—begun under former CEO Michael Eisner—to open Disneyland in Shanghai, is equally sensitized to the opportunity and complexity of landing and operating in China. And Facebook is not starting from scratch in the country. Although it is a little understood beachhead, Facebook already serves the Chinese market with a brisk business selling advertising to companies based in China—from its office in Hong Kong—who are promoting their products (most often mobile apps) elsewhere in the world.

Their effort to land a consumer product in China would be aided—as it has been for so many Western companies now operating in the country—by a partnership with a local company, and local investment via real estate, infrastructure, job creation and revenue sharing. One of the most interesting possibilities on this front would be a partnership with a telecommunications company such as China Telecom with whom Facebook could build telecommunications infrastructure and data centers using its open-sourced Open Compute and Telecom Infrastructure Project technologies and—without the complexities of net neutrality policy it would face in most other countries—offer a differentially priced Internet onboarding service that brings new awareness and long-term customers (there are still over 500 million unconnected Chinese) to China Telecom and new users to Facebook.

To actually deliver a compelling product, Facebook would need to leverage a unique asset to overcome the advantage of local players. Their best opportunity may be to deliver a modified version of the services it offers elsewhere that asserts their leadership in content from global celebrities, athletes and media companies and combines it with their expertise and technology in mobile video, including live broadcasts. Between Facebook and Instagram—whose contents Facebook could easily combine into one offering—the company has hundreds of sources of content with the most intense global consumer interest, including artists and entertainers (from Beyoncé to The Rock and Vin Diesel to John Cena), athletes and teams (from footballers Cristiano Ronaldo, Lionel Messi and Neymar and basketball players LeBron James and Kevin Durant to teams including Manchester United and FC Barcelona), and entertainment (from Disney to MTV and Red Bull to *The Simpsons*), each with tens of millions of global followers to which these producers are already communicating on a daily basis and who would welcome Facebook's efforts to extend their reach—especially via video—in China, the second largest economy in the world. While this service would not focus primarily on connections between people, it does offer a unique sense of connection beyond China that people there crave and would be fully stocked with more content than any other source—an archive, possibly even curated, of all the pictures and video previously posted—the day it launched.

As for censorship, in addition to the fact that these sources of content are less likely than the average user to run afoul of China's censorship due to their own commercial interests with consumers in the country, Facebook could use its advanced artificial intelligence (more on that in Chapter 13) to provide an enhanced ability to affect censorship not just via specific keyword filtering but on the more general meaning of writing, pictures and videos, a technical advance the Chinese government intent on proving its model of Internet sovereignty would likely value and promote as a victory. Enabling the Chinese government with this technology could be seen as a Faustian bargain, but is precisely the kind of complex decision that Zuckerberg will increasingly be faced with given the scale at which he is operating, and the progress or failure that will be at stake.

Other Long Games: Japan and India

Facebook is involved in two other long games also occurring in Asia under the watch of Regional Vice President Dan Neary, but the challenges of the two are different from China and each other.

At 120 million, **Japan**'s population is less than a tenth that of China, but its total advertising marketplace is the third most lucrative in the world behind only the United States and China. Projected to total $43 billion by 2018,[9] six times as much is spent on advertising per person in Japan as in China and 35 times as much as in India. That makes every additional Japanese user of Facebook's services very valuable, and although there are 25 million users of Facebook, that is only a 22% share of the 91% of Japanese already on the Internet and not a leadership position. Instagram has 8 million users and is growing quickly, but if patterns from other countries hold true in Japan, the audience has significant overlaps with Facebook rather than being incremental.

Facebook will not only have to contend with digital leaders like local messaging service Line (more than twice as big as Facebook), global Internet video leader YouTube and even Twitter (Japan is one of the few countries where Twitter's users exceed those of Facebook), but also the complexity of Japan's advertising business where TV is still the preferred medium at 43% share of the overall business (nearly twice the share of digital) and the ad buying process is controlled nearly monopolistically by powerful local advertising agency Dentsu, which has long-standing agreements with media properties and celebrities and a tight-knit network with Japan's big advertising spenders. Nevertheless, a doubling of each of Facebook's user penetration and per-person share of the advertising market in Japan could eventually be worth more than $1 billion annually.

Facebook's long game in Japan has been underway for many years and will have to continue for many more as no shortcuts are available. They have invested in consumer promotion of Facebook including TV ads and are counting on Instagram to be a powerful boost given how well aligned it is with the aesthetic emphasis in Japanese culture *and* advertising and that it does not have Facebook's real name policy, which doesn't always mesh with a more reserved Japanese culture.

The prize and challenge in **India** are entirely different from those of Japan. Not a particularly lucrative advertising market (projected to be a total of only $11 billion in 2018[10]), the opportunity in India is instead as a proving ground that Facebook can play a meaningful role in connecting the unconnected. With 1.25 billion inhabitants but only 30% Internet penetration, India is the single biggest incremental Internet connectivity opportunity in the world.

After missteps with internet.org and Free Basics (more in Chapter 14), Facebook will have to reset but can continue to draw on a reservoir of early success—India's 136 million Facebook users make it the second largest country on Facebook—via rapid introductions of new features and products and the will to make progress. Its remarkably bandwidth-efficient Facebook Lite has already found rapid success among the kind of users who are the next group to connect permanently, and infrastructure technologies meant to further reduce the costs of connectivity, like drones and dedicated satellites being tested in sub-Saharan Africa, will rapidly make their way to India if they show promise. While it may be Facebook's longest game of all and the one with the heaviest infrastructure lifting, Zuckerberg's ability to progress against the most fundamental aspect of his mission to make the world more connected is at stake. Expect a special brand of dogged effort.

Which Long Games to Play and When

The farther out one looks, the more options appear to present themselves, especially if you have found a measure of confidence from your early successes. That makes long games the most enticing, least concrete and most dangerous opportunities of all.

With billions of dollars of revenue and as a many as a billion new users of Facebook's services at stake over the next decade, China, Japan and India are very much long games but occupy a particular spot in the order of Facebook's priorities: they are dedicated to winning these efforts but can afford to lose without fundamental harm to the business.

To help make sense of the various kinds of efforts in a business, here is a framework of projects and degrees of criticality to aid in evaluating and planning:

- **Fundamental projects**: The basic expression of your mission

- **Adjacent projects**: A clear—not wishful—expansion of your mission

- **Essential**: A hill you cannot lose or the one from which competition could attack fatally

- **Nonessential**: Failure does not harm the business fundamentally

Figure 10.1 shows what some of Facebook's strategy to date looks like in that framing.

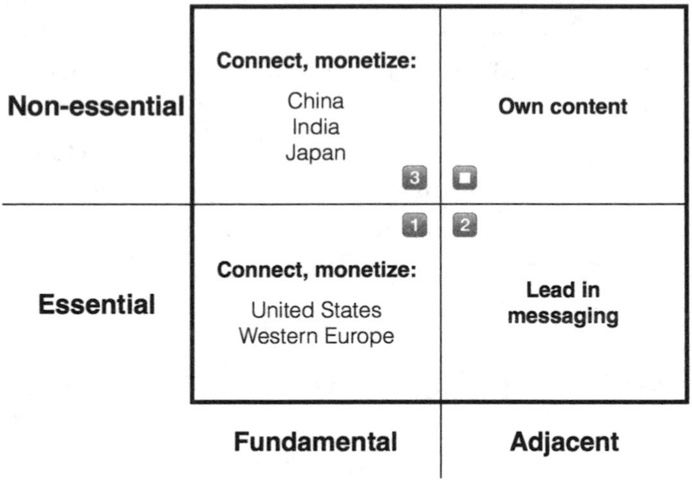

Figure 10-1. Framework for evaluating projects for prioritization

The majority of Facebook's effort, and its highest priority, during Facebook's first decade were connecting people in the United States and Western Europe and growing advertising revenue relative to those audiences. Connecting existing Internet users in markets accounting for about 50% of global advertising spend[11] is both fundamental to Facebook's mission and essential to its business.

When that effort was on a successful road, Zuckerberg turned his attention to the growing threat of the adjacent messaging market and consolidated the Facebook leadership position with the evolution of the homegrown service Messenger and the very sizable acquisition of WhatsApp (more on that in Chapter 13) in an area clearly adjacent to the core mission and, although not yet broadly lucrative from a revenue perspective, a hill from which others could have attacked Facebook's core business with dangerous consequences.

Only then did Zuckerberg increase the intensity with which Facebook treated China, Japan and India, but neither to the investment levels of the billions of dollars that had gone into the core of Facebook, Messenger and the acquisition of WhatsApp nor with the same expectations of success. Connecting people in China, Japan and India is certainly fundamental to Zuckerberg's mission and would bring additional revenue, but the business can survive the uncertainty inherent in these long games with no guarantee of winning.

What Zuckerberg has stayed away from entirely to date are projects that are neither fundamental nor essential. Efforts like owning content (e.g., acquiring the likes of Netflix or Viacom) barely fall within the broadest interpretation of making the world more open and connected and are not essential to a healthy advertising business.

Facebook's approach to the long game is worth emulating. Don't be afraid of long games, but take care of the essential part of the business first.

11

How Facebook Wins the Talent Wars

LESSON 9:

Employee engagement is everything. Fit to people's strengths and ignore weaknesses.

Background: With constant connectivity, our jobs have never felt more dangerously pervasive. At the same time, an increasingly service-oriented economy has driven the notion of people being a company's most important asset to ever greater heights. More than any other single factor, the degree of engagement people have with their company—and their work—affects their contributions and intent to stay.

Facebook's Move: Facebook puts an emphasis on connecting people to their most engaging work throughout the company, all the way up to its two most important leaders, Zuckerberg and Sandberg.

Thought Starter: When was the last time you asked the people around you what the best part of their day is?

The People Person

In the decade after getting her MBA from Harvard, Lori Goler had shown herself to be what Silicon Valley likes to call an "athlete," someone with a broad set of abilities in business that have played out in different environments. She had been in business planning at The Walt Disney Company, held general management responsibilities at dotcom-era babystyle.com and led consumer marketing at eBay for five years.

It's not surprising that when she reached out to Sheryl Sandberg in 2008, she began the call with the very open-ended question, "Sheryl, what is your biggest problem, and can I help solve it?" Sandberg—still in the first few months of her time at Facebook—quickly jumped to the steady stream of incoming talent the company would need in order to live up to its aspirations and asked Goler to come on board to run Recruiting.

It mattered little that Goler had never led a recruiting organization. She had a reputation as a talented exec, was excited about Facebook's mission and knew that the role mattered a great deal to the company. Just a few months into the job, Chris Cox who led the People team—what other companies call Human Resources—would move to lead the Product team and asked Goler to succeed him, expanding Goler's responsibilities to HR *and* Recruiting.

In the eight years since, Goler's most important contribution to Facebook has been her focus on being a "strengths-based" organization as it went from just a few hundred employees in 2008 to more than 12,000 in 2016, making Facebook and Goler perhaps the largest practitioner of the approach in the world and a consistent winner in the Silicon Valley talent wars.

Anatomy of the Talent Wars

Significant parts of Silicon Valley's talent wars play out very visibly above the surface in the form of headline-making transitions to Facebook by the likes of Sandberg, consumer marketing head Gary Briggs, advertising business leader David Fischer and leader of newly formed Building 8 skunkworks Regina Dugan (all from Google), Messenger head David Marcus (from PayPal), AI research lab leader Yann LeCun (from academia), and the post-acquisition arrivals of Instagram and WhatsApp CEOs Kevin Systrom and Jan Koum. Other parts play out on smaller stages with lesser-known players who are headhunted, acqui-hired (small acquisitions done primarily to bring on talent) or raise their hand to indicate availability. They may join partially because of the money—if they join early enough—but more so because of the irresistible scope of what they could affect with the things they might build at Facebook (if you're interested in a dark, borderline vindictive take on that story, read Antonio Garcia Martinez's soapy 2016 tell-all *Chaos Monkeys*).

But when you're hiring thousands of new people a year—all of whom still need to be the best of whoever remains outside of Facebook but don't rate a headline in *TechCrunch*, *Recode* or *AdAge*—and you can no longer offer world-altering degrees of control or life-altering stock grants, you need an attractor that works for everyone: a reputation for delivering job satisfaction not just for the rock stars but the rank and file.

And hiring is not the most important part. Keeping the 10,000 great employees you already have for as long as you can is the most important part. They are most familiar with what you're doing and how you're doing it. Their knowledge and learnings are the hardest to transition and replace. In the exceedingly fortunate economic and intellectual environment of Silicon Valley, which skews younger and, because of its constant creative destruction, values the last few years of your resume above all, the urge to move between opportunities—and the opportunity and encouragement to do so—is extreme. Staying a mere four years—the usual vesting period of initial stock grants that largely control personal outcomes—at one company is common in this twitchy environment. Six years is very good news for your employer, and anything over 10 years is cause for special celebrations. Without the nearly infinitely renewable source of energy that comes from a focus on employee engagement, companies have little chance of being a positive outlier in that distribution.

Attrition, however, is inescapable, so winning the talent wars—and with it your company's longevity—means winning the inflow vs. outflow equation: are you keeping employees longer than your ever-evolving competition, and are more people coming to you from those competitors than are leaving to join them?

The Inner Game of Employee Engagement

Going back to 1999, Goler had been a fan of Marcus Buckingham's and Curt Coffman's management tome *First, Break All the Rules*. Based on 25 years of Gallup studies of 80,000 managers at 400 companies, the book finds four commonalities among great frontline managers:

1. Select for talent, not just experience or determination.
2. Define outcomes, not steps.
3. Motivate by focusing on strengths, not fixing weaknesses.
4. Find the right fit, not just the next rung.

Numbers 1 and 2 are good, but numbers 3 and 4 most interest Goler: an organizational mindset that focuses on people's strengths and practically ignores their weaknesses (or, put slightly more pragmatically, works to make weaknesses irrelevant nontalents relative to someone's role). This focus is a big driver of people's engagement with their job and company, which in turn is a primary factor in their performance and intent to stay, the preeminent asset in the people economy of Silicon Valley.

Why is Goler so confident in the engagement-centric approach? It comes down to the chemistry of flow and the math of jungle gyms.

While intuitively it seems "nice" to match people's strengths to their roles in order to maximize engagement, the success of the practice goes much deeper than that. It is rooted in research begun in the 1970s at the University of Chicago by Hungarian psychologist Mihaly Csikszentmihalyi. Known simply as "flow," it refers to an optimal state of consciousness where we feel—and perform—our best. It's so powerful that in a 10-year study conducted by McKinsey, top executives reported being five times more productive in flow.

Csikszentmihalyi's work surfaces a specific approach to understanding how to get into flow and why it is such a powerful state: the flow channel. Depicted in the upper right of Figure 11-1, it relates your skill with a task to the challenge of that task. When you are skilled but not challenged, you are bored. When you are not skilled but highly challenged, you are anxious. When you are neither skilled nor challenged, you are apathetic. In the flow channel, however, you are finely balanced between a constant growth in an existing skill and a level of challenge slightly beyond that skill.

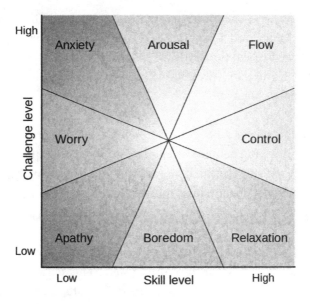

Figure 11-1. Mental states brought about by various combinations of skill and challenge

When in the fine balance of the flow channel, we feel focused, have inner clarity, higher confidence and greater creativity; we learn faster and have a sense of timelessness and high intrinsic motivation. If that sounds suspiciously like an altered state, that's because it is. Writing in *Harvard Business Review* in May 2014, Steven Kotler describes the rare confluence of neurochemicals:

> In flow, the brain releases norepinephrine, dopamine, endorphins, anandamide, and serotonin. Norepinephrine and dopamine tighten focus, helping us shut out the persistent distractions of our multi-tasked lives. Endorphins block pain, letting us burn the candle at both ends without burning out altogether. Anandamide prompts lateral connections and generates insights far more than most brainstorming sessions. And serotonin, that feel-good chemical . . . bonds teams together more powerfully than the best-intentioned offsite.

These five chemicals are the biggest rewards the brain can produce, and flow is one of the only times the brain produces all five simultaneously. This makes the state one of the most pleasurable, meaningful and— literally—addictive experiences available.

Good stuff, this flow. And having more of it at work is premised on Goler's focus: connecting people's strengths with their roles. Flow cannot be induced externally through edict or command. It is virtually impossible to establish without the intrinsic motivation of having your opportunity balanced with your capacity (in the context of clear goals and rapid feedback).

When teams and entire organizations can create these conditions at scale, flow can even exist for the entire system. This sense of group cohesion is known as "social flow," and at Facebook it stems from the tremendous buy-in to Facebook's mission of making the world more open and connected at all levels of the company.

In addition to chemistry, there is also math to employee engagement, and it is best captured by contrasting the traditional "career ladder" with Goler's favorite alternative, the "jungle gym" (her own career has been an example of not only lateral job moves but also steps down such as her original Facebook role).

If a feeling of engagement can be sustained only by constantly being promoted to higher levels of a pyramid with fewer spots at each successive step, the "ladder" makes it a certainty that engagement won't last for most employees. A "jungle gym," on the other hand, offers the flexibility of increasing personal development with greater accompanying challenges in one area, as well as the resetting to a new combination of interest, skill and challenge in another.

Put another way, there is simply more room on a jungle gym than on a ladder for everyone to keep flowing.

And that flow has proven crucial to people feeling that they are performing at their best for over 40 years of research across audiences as diverse as surgeons, musicians, dancers, climbers, chess players, Italian farmers,

Navajo sheep herders, elderly Korean women, Chicago assembly line workers and Japanese teenage gang members.

It is *particularly* relevant, however, to Millennials, who will become 44%—the largest part—of the American workforce by 2025[1] and believe to a much greater degree than Baby Boomers (91% to 71%) that "achieving success and recognition in a career is necessary to living a good life" and will move to the right employer to find the environment for that success (60% of them leave within three years of being hired).[2]

The implication for the future is simple: engagement that comes from matching skills and challenges isn't just a nice-to-have for the best companies in the world; it will be impossible to be best without it.

It Works . . . All the Way to the Top

Enough of the theory. Does it work?

Judging by data collected by compensation analysis firm Payscale in 2015 from 33,500 tech workers and published in March 2016, it works very well. Facebook employees were both the most satisfied (96%) and the least stressed (44%) of the 18 top technology companies that were the focus of the study. The next closest company, Google, had less than 90% satisfaction, and technology giant Apple barely more than 70%.

Additionally, Facebook is number 2 (and 1 in Technology), in anonymous job survey site Glassdoor's "Best Places to Work in 2017" with a rating of 4.5 out of 5 stars, 92% of employees likely to recommend the company to a friend, 92% of employees having a positive outlook for the company's future and 98% approving of Zuckerberg's leadership as CEO. Google is 4th. Apple 36th.

Although scoffed at by outsiders, conveniences such as free food, laundry service and shuttle buses have become so common in Silicon Valley that they are no longer the differentiator in the talent wars being waged here every day. A reputation for job satisfaction at a company-wide scale is often now the difference maker, and the reason that Facebook is winning the inflow vs. outflow math of the talent wars.

According to analysis by recruiting site Top Prospect as far back as 2011, Facebook was pulling employees from Apple 11 times more than

Apple from Facebook, held a 15:1 advantage over Google and 30:1 over Microsoft. Even in 2015, LinkedIn data examined by Quartz still showed that while Microsoft, Google and Apple were all in the top five former employers of current Facebook employees, Facebook did not appear in the top five list of former employers for Microsoft, Google and Apple employees.

One of the most institutionalized examples of the engagement-focused culture at Facebook is the practice of newly hired engineers selecting their chosen team—as opposed to the other way around—at the conclusion of the company's six-week Bootcamp that begins every engineer's time with the company.

Perhaps even more telling, the strengths-based approach plays out all the way to the top of the company, including the division of labor between Zuckerberg (who focuses nearly all his time on product strategy and development) and Sandberg (who is focused on operating the advertising business, partner ecosystems, communications and policy). Zuckerberg spends little time with advertising customers (in contrast to what you would see from more traditionally aligned CEOs), and Sandberg similarly little time on Facebook's consumer products. These are not signs of disinterest or disrespect for customers or products, respectively, but simply a maximization of the amount of time the duo spends in their areas of strength.

The practice gives Facebook, its employees and its customers the best possible outcomes, and Zuckerberg and Sandberg make for Goler's best role models for the strengths-based approach, reminding every employee to find their best fit and every manager to play an enabling role in the process.

12

How Facebook Became the Biggest of the Big

LESSON 10:
Care more.

Background: Significant change requires an unusual degree of day-in-and-day-out effort. Only an extraordinary degree of passion can fuel that effort.

Facebook's Move: Facebook succeeded—to even Zuckerberg's surprise—against giant competitors who were in a better position to deliver on the kind of services Facebook built because they cared more about delivering on their mission even in the midst of their most difficult moments. Today, over a billion people a day use Facebook.

Thought Starter: Does anyone care more about your mission than you?

The Terrible, Horrible, Very Bad, No Good 124 Days

A month after the well-received announcement of the Instagram acquisition—and still in the middle of their pre-IPO quiet period—things started to take a giant turn for the worse, and that's how we find ourselves back at the crossroads Facebook faced in Chapter 1.

If it had not been such a serious occasion under the hot lights of one of the most anticipated IPOs ever, the you-can't-make-this-up cavalcade of bad news followed by worse news would have been comically unbelievable.

On May 9, 2012, in the 6th amendment to their S1 registration document describing the public offering, Facebook committed one of the great acts of apparent self-incrimination when they added language to the prospectus less than 10 days before the IPO including this passage:

> We do not currently directly generate any meaningful revenue from the use of Facebook mobile products, and our ability to do so successfully is unproven. If users increasingly access Facebook mobile products as a substitute for access through personal computers, and if we are unable to successfully implement monetization strategies for our mobile users, or if we incur excessive expenses in this effort, our financial performance and ability to grow revenue would be negatively affected.

Not great. Uncertainty is damaging to any stock. More so if it's a highly watched stock. On the eve of its public market debut. And it's the company itself increasing the uncertainty.

Just a week later and a mere two days prior to the IPO, it would be auto manufacturer GM, the United States' third largest advertiser—and a Facebook customer rumored to have spent upward of $10 million on the platform the prior year—who added fuel to the uncertainty fire. In a *Wall Street Journal* story on the front page of the business section ominously titled "GM Says Facebook Ads Don't Pay Off," GM CMO Joel Ewanick expressed concerns about Facebook's effectiveness and indicated he would be pulling all spend from Facebook. Coming only two days after Forrester research analyst Nate Elliott had written a blog post suggesting that "companies in industries from consumer electronics to financial services tell us they're no longer sure Facebook is the best place to dedicate their social marketing budget—a shocking fact given the site's dominance among users" and six months after Sir Martin Sorrell, leader of WPP, the world's biggest advertising agency holding company, said he had "fundamental doubts about the ability to monetize social platforms," things were getting critical.

Instead of the long-awaited IPO on the morning of Friday May 18 relieving all of the pent-up anxiety, it made it worse. Much worse.

The primary—and you might argue only—function of a stock exchange like the NASDAQ on which Facebook elected to trade its shares is to rapidly and accurately clear transactions between buyers and sellers and to disseminate the information related to those trades rapidly and accurately to the parties and to all participants of the exchange. On that Friday, the NASDAQ failed in epic fashion to perform that very function as computer system issues stemming from unprecedented demand caused a 30-minute delay in the opening of Facebook stock and issues with Facebook trades completing and delivering notices of completion for over three hours following the opening. After 80 million shares traded in the first 30 seconds and 567 million over the course of the day, Facebook had set a record for volume exceeding even that of prior leader GM (yes, the same GM who was no longer a Facebook customer) but had paid a heavy price as the trading uncertainty, piled on top of the pent-up uncertainty during the IPO buildup, caused the stock to close at $38.23, below the days' opening price of $42, and ever so slightly above the IPO offering price of $38, only due to Facebook's own underwriting bankers supporting the stock late in the trading day by buying over 60 million shares of an overallotment to prop up the offering.

The NASDAQ's failure to handle the Facebook offering was so historic that 40 lawsuits would be filed and the exchange would eventually have to pay a $10 million penalty to settle U.S. Securities and Exchange Commission (SEC) charges related to the IPO, voluntarily repay $41.6 million to market-making institutions affected by the first-day problems and be required to pay $26.5 million to a class of retail investors after being found guilty of violating federal and state laws by not disclosing technology weaknesses in its IPO systems and failing to properly design and test them for the Facebook offering, the first time *ever* that a class of investors was able to sustain claims against an exchange for market disruption.

The hangover of the trading issues on Friday was in full effect immediately upon opening on Monday May 21, 2012 as a rush to sell the stock caused it to drop by over 10% in five minutes, triggering a so-called circuit breaker in the exchange that temporarily halts trading of a stock to attenuate steep declines. Facebook ended trading that Monday down 11%.

And the hits would keep on coming.

The very next day, only the 3rd day of public trading for Facebook, a Reuters news story alleged that analysts at Morgan Stanley, JPMorgan Chase and Goldman Sachs—Facebook's own IPO underwriters set to make nearly $200 million in fees on the sell side of the IPO—cut earnings forecasts in the middle of the IPO run-up in response to both the mobile revenue warnings from the S1 amendment and conversations between Facebook finance executives and the analysts; they communicated the reduced forecasts to large clients verbally but not to the public. The move, widely believed to be unprecedented in the IPO community, could have caused fundamental sentiment changes among institutional investors and an imbalance of information between institutional investors who were participating in the buy and sell sides of the stock prior to the IPO and retail investors who could participate only after the IPO. One class-action lawsuit relative to the issue was dismissed in 2015, and as of December 2015, two more were still making their way through the legal system.

May 2012 concluded with the arbiter of all things business, *The Wall Street Journal*, declaring the IPO a "fiasco." Not surprisingly, the stock continued a nearly monotonistic decline to its September 4, 2012 low of $17.73, having shed over half its IPO valuation of $100 billion.

What exactly was causing all this pessimism?

Among Internet stocks, one is esteemed above all others: GOOG. Google—and its eventual parent company Alphabet, Inc.—is the model of sustained and profitable revenue growth and has been a success since its 2004 IPO. By Q4 2011, Facebook had begun to suffer by comparison to its big brother on two critical dimensions that we can see clearly in Figure 12-1: significantly less revenue at the same company age and a lower rate of year-on-year revenue *growth* to boot. Not a good combination. Not good at all.

By the time Zuckerberg stepped onto the stage at the TechCrunch Disrupt conference on September 11, 2012, for a fireside chat with notori-

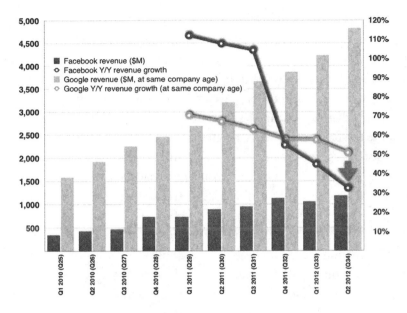

Figure 12-1. Facebook and Google revenue and revenue growth at same age as a company[1]

ously tough inquisitor Michael Arrington to make his first public comments since the IPO, concern over Facebook's future had reached a fever pitch and the hints of schadenfreude that float in the air when a former innovation darling struggles were palpable.

The venue was standing room only. And they were in for a surprise.

Pulling Up, Way Up

At the time, Zuckerberg was not known as a compelling public stage presence—in contrast to the success he enjoyed with his direct and thoughtful internal weekly Q&As at Facebook. The image etched in most outside observers' minds was the flop-sweat opening to his June 2010 All Things Digital conference interview with elite Silicon Valley journalists Kara Swisher and Walt Mossberg that covered lightning rod issues like privacy and was immortalized on allthingsd.com's liveblog this way: "My god, Zuckerberg is literally dissolving in a lake of his own sweat. Could this be his Nixon moment?"

In that context—and in the midst of *significantly* bigger challenges than even those of 2010—Zuckerberg's effortless, energetic and genuine discussion of Facebook's missteps and opportunities with Arrington in September 2012 was a revelation.

TechCrunch Facebook beat writer Josh Constine captured the moment: "Zuckerberg outlined his strategy with such depth and bravado that the typically fierce ... Arrington seemed pressed back on his heels."

Zuckerberg had been *direct* ("This is not the first up-and-down we've ever had"), *honest* ("The biggest mistake we made as a company is betting too much on [underperforming mobile technology] HTML5 as opposed to [faster] native [code]"), *prophetic*—about both revenue ("Our mobile strategy is fundamentally misunderstood. On mobile we're going to make a lot more money than on desktop") and talent ("It's a good time to join and great time to stick around")—and *resolute* ("I would rather be under-estimated. It gives us freedom to go out and do interesting stuff"). Like a fighter pilot on the edge of disaster still able to execute his duties with skill and calm, Zuckerberg had explained—with confidence as unassailable as it was unexplainable under the circumstances—how Facebook was pulling out of its dive.

This, however, was no "performance." It was merely Zuckerberg's first public reflection of the work that had been happening at Facebook for over a year: the complete rewrite of the crucial Facebook mobile app in high-performance native code for Apple's iOS (and four months later Google's Android), which doubled the number of News Feed items consumed on mobile per person and completed the company's pivot to mobile-first product development, the momentous decision to have ads in News Feed at all and the even bigger decision to extend this to the mobile News Feed. Work that over the following four years would grow a business in excess of $20 billion annual revenue from $0.

The response to Zuckerberg's discussion was overwhelmingly positive, both in the packed conference hall and on Wall Street where Facebook's stock was up as much 4.6% in the hours after his remarks. It would be the beginning of one of the great reversals of fortune in technology as the stock recovered to $23.23 on October 24, 2012, the day after the Q3 2012 earnings announcement showed an arrest of the declining revenue growth, to $34.36—nearly double its low point—on July 25, 2013, the day after the Q2 2013 earnings announcement continued to show revenue growth acceleration, to $42.66—the first time it had exceeded its IPO day opening price—on September 5, 2013 and to $57.96 on Christmas Eve 2013. By May 2016, it had more than doubled up that number again, reaching $120 and making Facebook worth nearly $350 billion, *seven times the value at its low point.*

In an irony that brings this period full circle, GM returned to advertising on Facebook in April 2013, following CMO Ewanick's departure in July 2012 (according to GM, Ewanick had "failed to meet the expectations the company has of an employee" related to improprieties in a seven-year $559 million sponsorship deal with English football club Manchester United).[2]

Figure 12-2 revisits the comparison to Google's business fundamentals to understand Facebook's recovery: the key to Facebook's success was a rare reacceleration in year-on-year revenue growth, going from a low of 32% in Q2 2012 to as high as 72% in Q1 2014, followed by another reacceleration to 52% in Q1 2016, a rare feat for a 12-year-old company with nearly $20 billion of annual revenues.

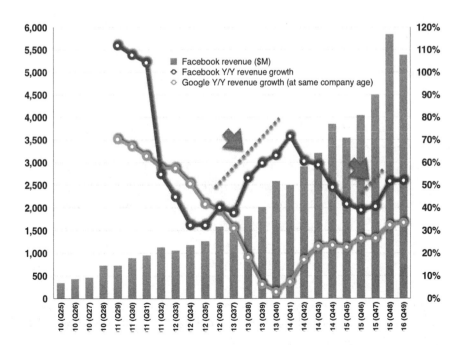

Figure 12-2. Facebook and Google revenue and revenue growth revisited

That historic bellwether Facebook had lagged in revenue growth in Q2 2012? Facebook has exceeded Google's historical growth rate at the same company age *every* quarter since Q4 2012 and closed a nearly four-year stretch with an impressive beat of earnings expectations in Q1 2016, the same week standard-bearers Alphabet *and* Apple disappointed. As Facebook's stock rose and Alphabet's and Apple's fell in the wake of those announcements, it marked a change of nearly $100 billion in valuation among the three critical consumer technology players in just *one* week.

Make no mistake, this revenue success—and the corresponding stock market success—is not a nice-to-have. It is central to Facebook's ability to create the kind of respect, confidence and enthusiasm that retains and attracts employees, customers and users. It is the life-giving oxygen on which the expansion of Facebook's core business relies and that makes possible the large acquisitions and investments that protect Facebook's future.

Internet-based consumer technologies live in a constant state of knife-edge inflection: up or down, there is no flat. Without the revenue growth turnaround begun in 2012, Facebook would be on the path of MySpace, Groupon, Yahoo and—more recently—Twitter.

Instead, it has become, by many measures, the biggest consumer service ever.

Just How Big Is Facebook?

More impressive even than Facebook's business performance between 2012 and 2016 is its growth as a provider of the things we cannot live without: it is the unquestioned leader in engaging consumer communication services on the medium of choice the world over—mobile.

In places like the United States, time spent on digital media began to exceed perennial champ traditional TV—which had a 60-year run—in 2013.[3] As we can see in Figure 12-3, the time spent on *mobile* devices alone is trending to take over television in 2020. This is especially true the younger you are. In the United States, for example, 18- to 24-year-olds spend 120+ hours per month on mobile.[4]

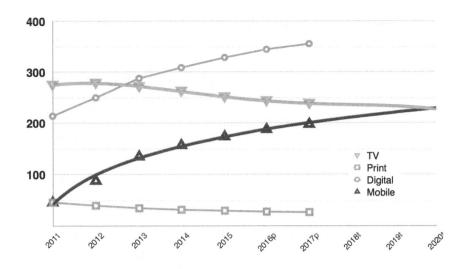

Figure 12-3. Average time spent per day for U.S. adults (minutes)

As we can see in Figure 12-4, among all that time spent on smartphones, *half* goes to people's most used app, and 80% of all time goes to the top three most used apps. In the United States, Facebook is the app used by most people (as it is in most countries). For 48% of its users,

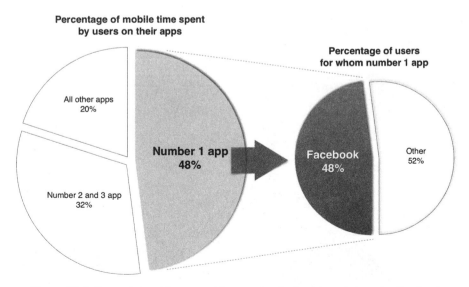

Figure 12-4. Percentage of time spent by users on their apps and share for Facebook

Facebook is the most used app on their phones, and for a full 80% of its users it is in the top three most-used.[5] The breadth and depth of its mobile usage is entirely without precedent.

The app used second most by people in the United States? Messenger, also from Facebook.

How much time do we spend with Facebook's products? In the United States, nearly *one of every four* minutes on mobile is spent on Facebook, Instagram and Messenger, adding up to *50 minutes per day* for their users.[6]

As we can see in Figures 12-5 and 12-6, Facebook's lead over the competition in both *how many* people use it and *how much* they use it makes for strange charts. There it is in the far upper right-hand corner. Whether for audiences 18–34 (where it has a 50% greater penetration than the next biggest service, which is Facebook-owned Instagram, and triple the engagement per person) or 35-and-over (where it has nearly five times higher engagement per person), Facebook has a lion's share of our attention.[7]

Around the world, as of December 2016, the company served more than 1.8 billion people on Facebook, over 1 billion on WhatsApp, over 1 billion on Messenger and more than 600 million on Instagram every month. On August 24, 2015, Facebook alone first served 1 billion people globally in a single day. Now, that number exceeds 1.2 billion.

Every. Single. Day.

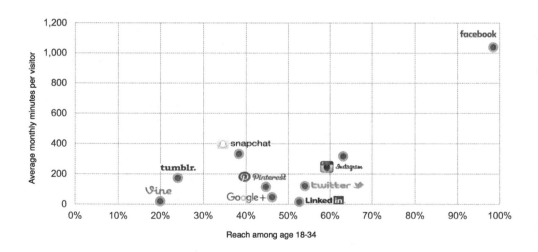

Figure 12-5. Age 18–34 digital audience penetration vs. engagement of leading social networks

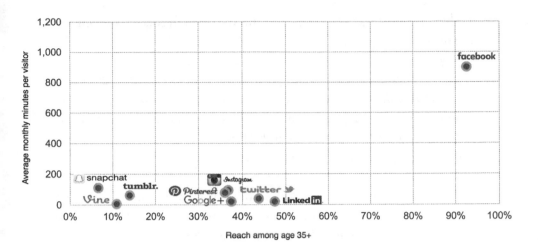

Figure 12-6. Age 35+ digital audience penetration vs. engagement of leading social networks

Caring More:
Getting Their Start at Pinocchio's

Few people are more surprised than Zuckerberg at Facebook's gigantic success in connecting people. Not because he doubted the mission. He doubted that the small band of people who started working on thefacebook.com back in 2004 could accomplish the feat at global scale before a larger and more usual suspect—he thought it would be Microsoft or Google—beat them to it. Back then, Zuckerberg and his contemporaries, including Harvard computer science classmate and longtime Facebook engineering leader Kang-Xing "KX" Jin, would huddle at Pinocchio's Pizza & Subs, a hole-in-the-wall joint a block off Boston's Harvard Square, to discuss the world. Connecting people was important and would happen, they agreed, but it would be somebody much bigger than their fledgling enterprise that would build the necessary services.

How, then, *did* Facebook win?

Zuckerberg, reflecting in comments he made on Facebook's 10th anniversary in 2014, believes that along the journey he and the ever-growing band aligning with his mission "just cared more about connecting people than anyone else."

In case "cared more" sounds too generic—or even corny—for you, let me offer a deeper interpretation: it is shorthand for being more focused (on growth and products through stagnations, existential questions, competitive threats, the withering microscope of people and the press and IPO distractions), faster, more eager to take risk and less afraid of failure, less burdened by the-way-it's-been-done and less coddled by the success of an existing business. All the things that allow a smaller competitor to turn the size of a larger competitor against them and breathe more life into connecting people than any company had before.

That Zuckerberg doesn't *appear* emotional about it is just a reminder that caring more doesn't always look the same. In that pivotal interview with TechCrunch in September 2012, Arrington's final question to Zuckerberg at the most difficult time the company had ever faced was whether he was still having fun. "Yeah," said Zuckerberg with a half-smile. Then he looked into the middle distance and concluded, "For me it's not really about fun though. It's about mission."

3

The Future

Messaging Becomes the Medium

Two more giant apps and an artificial intelligence based on trillions of pieces of data

Social media is big. So big that there is only one class of apps bigger: messaging. As you can see in Figure 13-1, while Facebook is the largest social network and Instagram the second largest, there are four messaging apps larger than Instagram: WhatsApp, Facebook Messenger and Chinese juggernaut Tencent's QQ and WeChat. A dominant seven of the top 10 communication apps in the world are now messaging apps.

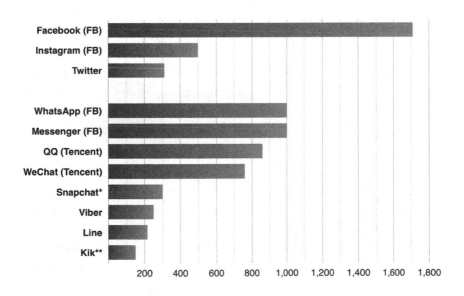

Figure 13-1. Global monthly users (millions, circa Q4 2015 to Q2 2016)[1]

Is it really possible that the *new* New Thing™ looks like the *old* New Thing™—think AOL's AIM and ICQ—from 20 years ago? It's not so surprising. Messaging has always been the first and foundational use of every two-way medium:

- ▶ **Telegraph (1844):** Samuel Morse's "What hath God wrought?"

- ▶ **Telephone (1876):** Alexander Graham Bell's "Mr. Watson, come here."

- ▶ **Internet (1969):** Charley Kline's "lo" (of "login")

Messaging is the *original* interface. We've been talking one-on-one and in small groups for tens of thousands of years, and our modern phones are perfectly suited to expand the pace and scale of that messaging:

- ▶ Messaging is the simplest, most human, function on our devices.

- ▶ Thanks to your contact list of phone numbers, messaging apps have an instant network of everyone you want to connect with.

- ▶ Everyone is available, all the time, but without the interruption of a phone call.

- ▶ In addition to bypassing operators' SMS/MMS fees—especially internationally—many Internet messaging apps also offer voice and video calling.

Because of these simple and powerful benefits, mobile messaging apps can grow quickly. QQ and WeChat (both belonging to Chinese Internet giant Tencent) did so in China, Line is the most popular service in Japan, Viber has a following in Europe and Snapchat is a favorite with U.S. Millennials.

Global leader WhatsApp grew to 400 million monthly active users in just four years. It took Facebook six.

Even following Facebook's acquisition of Instagram in 2012, it was clear that messaging was going to play a big role in how people shared and which apps were making the world more open and connected, the pursuit Facebook wanted—and needed—to lead. Whether messaging would someday become more prevalent than Facebook itself or simply continue to be adjacent, Zuckerberg needed to protect Facebook against an incursion on its mission while also finding access to additional business opportunities that early efforts by some messaging apps—particularly those in Asia—were beginning to grow to hundreds of millions of dollars.

Zuckerberg *needed* a dog in the messaging fight.

Dogs in the Fight

While one dog would be good, two would be better. And so begins the story of how the biggest dog of them all, and the one that started as an awkward puppy in Facebook's own backyard, wound up with the same owner.

It's not hard to understand where Jan Koum's low-key, pragmatic style comes from. Koum arrived in Silicon Valley in 1992 as a 16-year-old immigrant from communist Ukraine. He worked at a grocery store, collected food stamps and lived with his mother who suffered from cancer and eventually died in 2000. His father had not been able to come to the United States and died back in Ukraine in 1997.

He would start at San Jose University but leave before finishing his degree to work in infrastructure at Yahoo, where he met Brian Acton who would be a key partner throughout Koum's career. Disillusioned by the beginning of Yahoo's decline, the two left in 2007 and cast about for their next jobs, both—ironically—being rejected by Facebook. It was Koum's first iPhone—and the realization of the power of overlaying your contacts list with a simple and reliable Internet-based status and messaging capability—that drove him and Acton to launch WhatsApp in November 2009.

By early 2012—WhatsApp had 90 million active users—Zuckerberg reached out to Koum, and the two began to have regular meetings. *This* is the part where the Instagram acquisition and, more importantly, its post-acquisition success play a huge role.

As different as the matter-of-fact, under-the-radar Koum and the stylish and public Kevin Systrom are, they are both builders with vision who want a smart partner they've learned to trust and the resources and air cover of a successful business, but they also want to be largely left alone to move their products forward.

So when it came time for Koum to consider the $19 billion acquisition—

and a Facebook board seat—that Zuckerberg offered in a one-on-one conversation at his house in February 2014 after building the relationship for two years, Koum and Acton would agree.

By February 2016, two years after the acquisition was announced, WhatsApp would grow from 450 million monthly users to 1 billion and send more than 42 billion messages daily—more than double the number of all SMS messages globally—in addition to 1.6 billion photos and 250 million videos. All with a stunningly efficient 57 engineers.

While the story of WhatsApp is meteoric, Facebook Messenger, its home-grown messaging offering, is more of a meandering walkabout to greatness.

Although we've been able to send messages within Facebook since its beginnings on the web—something Facebook tried but failed to extend by combining texts, instant messages and e-mail with @facebook.com addresses in November 2010—they did not launch the stand-alone Messenger mobile app until August 2011, a move made possible by the acquisition of iOS and Android group messaging app Beluga earlier that year.

By November 2012, Messenger had grown to only about 57 million monthly users,[2] trailing messaging apps like WhatsApp and WeChat, which were rumored to have closer to 200 million users. So Facebook continued its split personality on messaging by integrating some of the best features of stand-alone Messenger back into its main Facebook app to play defense. Messenger continued to grow but by November 2013 was still not a breakout hit, so Facebook reworked the app to be a completely dedicated mobile-to-mobile one-to-one and small-group messenger obsessed with speed and ease of use, including the ability to connect with people based entirely on users' phone numbers instead of having to be a registered Facebook user—thus mirroring the simple mechanism by which most other large messaging apps made connections.

Six months later, Messenger was still only at 200 million monthly users, and so in April 2014 Facebook made the fateful decision to remove all messaging functionality from its main Facebook app and force people to download Messenger, a controversial move at the time.

Having just made one very big decision regarding Messenger in April, Zuckerberg made another one in May: he would reach out to the president of a 15,000-person company to build a relationship and convince him to come work for him to guide Messenger, a team of just 100 at the time.

David Marcus is a lifelong founder and builder of telecommunications and commerce offerings. In 1996, at age 23, he started GTN Telecom, one of the first telecommunications operators in Switzerland's deregulated market, and sold it to consolidator World Access in 2000. He then started Echovox, a mobile monetization platform from which he would spin out Zong, a mobile payments company acquired by global Internet payment giant PayPal in 2011. At PayPal he became the leader of mobile and, in 2012, its president.

In short, Marcus was the perfect person to take on the task of building Messenger into something very big now that its is-it-or-isn't-it-part-of-the-Facebook-app schizophrenia was behind it. The evolution of Instagram and WhatsApp, the opportunity to focus on *building* the now accelerating Messenger instead of *maintaining* PayPal and Facebook's overall growth and business success proved a heady cocktail that Zuckerberg offered up over multiple one-on-one sessions and that eventually Marcus could not resist.

In August 2014, Marcus became the fourth giant builder, along with Instagram's Kevin Systrom, WhatsApp's Jan Koum and Oculus VR's Brendan Iribe, to join Facebook in a period of two and a half years.

It would prove a good decision as the independence of Messenger was paying massive dividends. It grew to 500 million monthly users by November 2014, to 800 million by the end of the following year and to 1 billion by July 2016, giving Facebook not just one but *two* platforms serving more than 1 billion people in the crucial messaging future.

A question that sometimes arises when looking at the two messaging products in Facebook's stable is whether Zuckerberg really needs both of them. Aside from the two apps creating a belts-and-suspenders hedge in an important space and the strategic flexibility to have Messenger play a pathfinding role in the business aspects of messaging while WhatsApp continues to focus primarily on user growth, it turns out that the two are *very* complementary when looking at their leadership in the category across some of the biggest Internet countries around the world by the end of 2015. As you can see in Table 13-1, while WhatsApp dominates in Latin America and Africa, Messenger leads in the United States. The two split popularity across European and Asian countries. Only Russia, China, Japan and South Korea have escaped their grasp to date.

	WhatsApp Is Number 1	Messenger Is Number 1	Neither Is Number 1
United States and Canada	Canada	U.S.	
Latin America	Brazil Mexico Argentina		
Europe	Germany Turkey Spain Italy	UK France	Russia (Skype)
Africa	Nigeria Egypt		
Asia Pacific	India Indonesia	Phillipines Vietnam Thailand Australia	China (QQ, WeChat) Japan (Line) S. Korea (KakaoTalk)

Table 13-1. Leading messaging apps around the world

On the Cusp of Something Even Bigger

As big as messaging is, it's likely a predecessor to something bigger still.

What if messaging were more than messaging? What if instead of just sending messages to people, we could easily include app-like features in our messages ("This is the song I was talking about this morning.")? What if instead of messaging just with *people*, we could message with *things* ("Show me the two best options for European river cruises.")? What if over time those things could become as intelligent as people and do work on our behalf ("I noticed you were making plans to visit Melanie in Austin next week; here are two restaurants in Austin both of you might like. I can make reservations.")? What if a group made up of people and intelligent things could converse and get things done together ("We need to pull the data about the best-performing Q2 marketing programs and develop the Q4 plan accordingly.")? What if this kind of messaging supersedes mobile apps the way mobile apps superseded the web?

What if the graphical user interfaces of the last 30 years were just a stopgap on the way back to the future of the "original" interface: natural language?

An interactive *thing* participating in messaging is known as a "bot." The simplest version of this is taking an action you've previously done using an app and instead using messaging as a platform to request and deliver that action. These are available today, especially with voice-based interfaces, from some of the biggest Internet players: Apple's Siri ("What was the score of last night's Warriors' game?"), Google's Now ("What's next on my calendar?") and Amazon's Echo ("Reorder my favorite Keurig cups").

Already some existing messenger apps like Telegram and Kik for consumers and Slack for business users are acting as platforms that allow other services to plug into their environment to deliver existing services via a messaging interface. Some, like Assist, are building standalone bots to deliver simple services like hailing a ride, getting food delivery, making restaurant reservations and sending flowers. Atlantic Media's Quartz has built a dedicated app that brings you the news in a messaging-like environment. Others, including Operator and Magic, are using messaging interfaces backed by a combination of software *and* people to deliver services.

To go much beyond these basic bots will require one of the great evolutions in all of computing: the intelligence, knowledge, history, anticipation and efficiency of a personal assistant. A digital mash-up of beloved *Downton Abbey* housekeeper Mrs. Hughes and butler Mr. Carson, James Bond boss M's assistant Ms. Moneypenny and trusty *West Winger* Mrs. Landingham.

While the wide open and natural way of messaging—say anything—works fantastic for *people* who are particularly adept at deciphering meaning and applying it to their sophisticated understanding of other people and the world, it is notoriously difficult for *computers*. It would, however, be an immense force-multiplier for people to get computers involved in working on our behalf without the constrained environments of today's interfaces—click here, select this, scroll there, enter that, read this—so the best and the brightest press on to evolve these interfaces. To do so, they need to make advances in the broad and complex field of artificial intelligence.

Which means Zuckerberg would need one more big asset beyond two giant messaging platforms to be best positioned for the future: a world-class artificial intelligence lab and an icon to run it.

How fortunate that back in December in 2013 he had recruited—once again via building a relationship and using the scale of Facebook's mission and the bona fides of Facebook's existing growth and success of the Instagram integration—pioneering artificial intelligence researcher Yann LeCun. The 55-year-old Frenchman started his path to legend in the early 1990s when he pioneered the use of so-called convolutional neural networks in the field of deep learning. Those fancy words refer to using computers to imitate the way networks of neurons in systems like the human visual cortex work. They are a way for *very* literal machines to be *somewhat* abstract. To recognize new things that are similar—but not identical—to many known things that have been given to the computer and internalized at gigantic scale in its preferred language of bits, numbers and math.

Computers may not *reason* easily, but they are *very* good at ingesting data and doing math. Given enough data, they can slowly form an understanding of the world. Especially if it's data like Facebook's trillions of objects and associations.

The appeal of that data and opportunity to start and lead a team of researchers in California, London, Paris and his native New York while remaining on the faculty at New York University were enough to add LeCun to the mix of great minds at Facebook trying to make the world more open and connected.

LeCun's research group creates the foundational progress that the applied teams elsewhere at Facebook turn into products for you and me:

▸ **Facial recognition**: To make it easier to tag your family and friends

▸ **Image recognition**: To make Facebook more accessible for the vision impaired

▸ **Video recognition**: To aid in classification—Facebook's algorithms are smart enough to identify automatically something as obscure as mountain unicycling—and compression

▶ **Language translation**: To help you understand your French Canadian friends

▶ **Text analysis**: To understand the content, sentiment and meaning of status updates in conjunction with photos and videos and assist the News Feed algorithm in selecting the most relevant content for you

Courtesy of the relentless march of performance improvements—and cost reduction—in computing, as well as the Facebook infrastructure team's ability to fashion them into powerful digital factories, the most common form of machine intelligence—supervised learning—is reaching a very accomplished stage. The scale and speed at which we can teach computers about language, images and video have made computer *recognition* commonplace.

So, onward we go to the more complex problems: meaning, reasoning, planning, prediction and remembering. This is the domain of *unsupervised* learning, something that humans do naturally and literally 24×7 from birth but that is more difficult for computers as it involves constant observation, comprehending relationships between things and the maintenance and constant evolution of lots and lots of memory and *understanding.*

The difference between supervised learning and unsupervised learning is the difference between understanding a picture and understanding *you.*

Put more abstractly, Facebook's computing power is the brain, and all of us the senses of a machine working to understand the world as a whole and each of us individually. What is so pedestrian to people will be the pinnacle for computing: common sense.

That may all seem far-fetched to us in 2017, but just 10 years ago it was equally inconceivable that each of us would carry in our pockets a screen that is connected to everyone and everything we care about. Everywhere. All the time.

When you put all of Facebook's state-of-the-art-in-2016 assets together—including January 2015 speech recognition acquisition wit.ai—

you get the beginnings of something bigger than just a mobile version of AOL Instant Messenger: Facebook M, a virtual assistant that uses the Messenger interface and is backed by artificial intelligence that has—and this is the important part to bridge from today's capabilities to tomorrow's—*human* trainers behind it. Instead of relying just on people, which would never scale to a billion users, or just on computers, which aren't consistently smart enough yet to take care of things for you by themselves, M's artificial intelligence will take its best first cut at dealing with your requests, and its human trainers will supervise the work and make the final decisions in handling your requests while the AI observes—and learns. It's like *Training Day* for computers. And unlike a real call center where the more people it serves, the worse it gets, with M, the more people it serves, the smarter it gets.

The eventual aim of M is far beyond asking Siri about the weather. It is to use advances in language understanding, vision, prediction and planning to create a Messenger-based digital personal assistant to take care of things for each of us, so we can spend more time on the thing computers cannot do for us: being human.

One Version of the Future: Conversational Interfaces

As we look toward a possible future where messaging platforms are the new browsers (or stores) and bots the new sites (or apps), isn't there a chance that we are taking three ease-of-use steps back to the cryptic days of "command lines" before graphical user interfaces (GUI) came along? Isn't the lack of mass adoption of voice-based assistants like Apple's Siri a sign that even though we *can* do these things, not enough of us actually *will*? Aren't the constraints of a GUI meant to guide us through the few things we can do next, as opposed to overwhelming us with the unlimited possibilities of an empty text entry box? How will I know what that empty box can do unless it can do *everything*? Is the magic of a digital assistant understanding one request ruined by its inability to understand the next?

To navigate the biggest interface evolution since the arrival of GUIs, we will have to keep the best of the past and bring in the best of what's now possible: a combination of GUIs and messaging interfaces where you will have the simple back-and-forth, natural language interface you enjoy with other people, and bots—initially backed by people—will respond with graphical, interactive objects contextual to the task you're completing. We will go through a long transition from highly structured conversations—think the choose-your-own-adventure mechanic of a few options along each step of the conversation—to increasingly free-form interactions, to a truly open conversation with meaning, memory, prediction and anticipation.

All of it following the rapid evolution of unsupervised machine learning backstopped by human trainers until that fateful day when we can finally take the training wheels off and watch bots like M ride into the future by themselves.

Alongside Facebook, other big Internet players in this evolution with the necessary relationship with people—and the data and technology to understand them progressively better—are Google, Amazon (especially in commerce) and Apple (especially in entertainment).

Is There a New Business in This Future?

Definitely. And not just because WeChat's mobile commerce to order a taxi or pay for a movie or Line's special business accounts to enable direct messaging with consumers are already making hundreds of millions of dollars.

With Messenger as the lead dog sniffing out opportunities so that WhatsApp can continue to focus on user growth and learn from Messenger's discoveries, Zuckerberg now has two more assets to create opportunities for people and businesses to connect.

However, finding revenue opportunities that continue the trend of creating value for both people and businesses is not as simple as bringing the Facebook and Instagram advertising experience to messengers since it does not fit the model of one-to-one or small-group messaging.

Instead, it will be communication in a context set by the user (although Facebook ads can be used to encourage people to reach out to businesses via messaging, thus bridging Facebook's advertising and messaging experiences):

▸ **Initial engagement**: [Bot] "You have a new meeting in Los Angeles in May. Can we help you with your travel arrangements?"

▸ **Assistance**: [You] "I need a better coffee maker than the one in this picture."

▸ **Transaction**: [You] "Order more diapers and the best crib toy for our baby girl."

▸ **Service**: [Bot] "Unfortunately, weather in Denver will cause you to miss your connecting flight, but we have rescheduled you on tomorrow morning's flight, made reservations at the Marriott and ordered an Uber to take you to the hotel."

▸ **Support**: [You] "My dishwasher is broken. Can you send someone?"

A new model for handling people's needs that plays out entirely in a single conversational graphical user interface rather than a convoluted nest of web searches, websites, mobile apps and phone calls. It may take a handful of years to mature—not unlike Facebook's advertising offering—but we are headed for a future of "agents" that are more powerful and easier to use than their app, website and phone support predecessors.

And as Facebook did for advertising, they will democratize this intelligent messaging over time for every business from the biggest airline to the smallest bakery and for every person with Internet access from the New York business traveler to the Indonesian fisherman expanding their economic network. They will know the most about people, the most about businesses, and provide the best artificial intelligence to assist the two in engaging with each other.

They will deliver Ms. Moneypenny as a service.

14

Connecting the
Next Billion People

*The most questionable business decision
for the best reasons*

Imagine Making this Pitch to Your Board:

I know we're still 25% below our IPO stock price and barely
have the advertising engine accelerating again in developed
markets, but I want to engage in a project that will cost hundreds and hundreds of millions of dollars annually for an
unknown length of time in areas we have little proven experience so that we can develop new technologies most of
which we will—assuming we overcome the high risk of failure—give away to telecommunications operators known to
be some of the most difficult partners in the technology ecosystem in places in the world we understand the least from a
cultural and regulatory perspective with the strong chance
of not producing appreciable returns for many years and
even under the best of circumstances, only being guaranteed
to acquire our least profitable future customers worth less
than a 10th of those in the United States.

That's essentially what Zuckerberg proposed to his board in early 2013 as
he set out to connect the rest of the world via new hardware, software,
services and partnerships.

It is the kind of quixotic undertaking that would be most CEOs' and
boards' fiduciary responsibility to *not* do.

Luckily, Zuckerberg has structural control over his board that precludes his being beholden to their vote—not to mention that his board of disruption-minded and forward-looking leaders has an appetite for exactly the kind of world-altering effort he was proposing—so the project dubbed internet.org went ahead.

That spring, he laid out his vision internally. The plan had had so little detailed analysis over the December 2012 holidays that certain quantitative elements would wind up being off by an order of magnitude. That could not have mattered less. It proved a brilliant elevating of the sights he was setting the company on to combat any potential letdown after the holy-sh*t-we-somehow-made-it-to-a-billion-users moment everyone had enjoyed in October 2012. Connecting *everyone* was an obviously greater and more worthy goal than a mere 1 billion. No matter how impossible it might have seemed, he successfully made the entire company believe that being the largest service in the world was merely the beginning.

Before we take a closer look at *how* he would try to do this, let's take a step back.

Why?[1]

Connecting the world falls into the category of challenges—peace, hunger, poverty, healthcare, education—so obviously important but so complicated, so large-scale and so widespread that they become overwhelmingly abstract to the average person. They are the kinds of problems in the face of which most of us can only offer tokens of support and a furrowed brow. Their scope is hard to fathom, with meaningful solutions so clearly beyond our individual means.

You could argue that connectivity is actually a challenge in a class of its own. A problem with disproportional leverage that, if summarily addressed, could contribute to addressing all other challenges in this category. Education and healthcare benefit from access to information. Poverty can be addressed in turn through education and connecting more people into the digital fabric of jobs and trading that is the increasingly global village.[2] Hunger is attacked through decreased poverty. And as a species we have to believe that peace—the canonical unsolvable challenge—is at least nudged forward by a more open and connected world.

Getting—and keeping—someone "on the grid" involves a series of costs and complexities. From the phone in your hand to the wireless antennae infrastructure (or base stations) that has to densely dot the world around you (at a radius of a few hundred feet for WiFi or a few miles for cellular telephony like 3G and 4G, in the United States alone, there are over 300,000 such cell sites installed at a cumulative capital expenditure of over $460 billion,[3] to say nothing of annual operational expenses that have likely pushed total investment over the past three decades in the United States over the trillion dollar mark) to the land-based connections from the wireless infrastructure (or backhaul), which often account for the majority of costs for a local provider and carry data on small tributaries to and from ever larger Internet connection and routing facilities (or Internet exchange points) to the main arteries (or backbone) of the Internet that simultaneously carry trillions of bits of information across countries and oceans in the form of light riding impossibly thin optical fibers.

It is these costs and complexities that cause the gap between the haves and have-nots in connectivity around the world to be as wide as 10 times: Internet penetration among the population of the most developed countries like the Netherlands, Denmark and Norway exceeds 95%, but is below 10% in a group of the least developed countries with a total population of 900 million.

Approximately 4 billion people in the world are not on the Internet as of 2015, with the weakest penetration in South Asia (only 17% of 1.4 billion people) and sub-Saharan Africa (only 19% of 800 million people). Out of that group, 1.4 billion have mobile phones but no data plan, making them the nearest opportunity for addressing the challenge, but 2.6 billion don't have a phone—and 1.1 billion don't even live on the electrical grid—making them most exposed to the connectivity divide. (See Figure 14.1.)

Two specific groups are disproportionately disadvantaged by the connectivity challenge:

▸ **Rural**: Rural network sites are two to three times as expensive to install and manage as urban sites (due primarily to the 10-fold

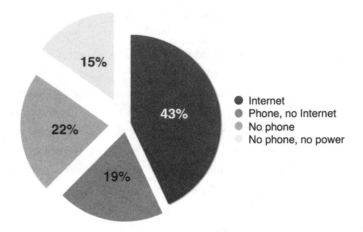

Figure 14-1. State of infrastructure for the world's population

increase in the cost of so-called backhaul connectivity—usually underground cables—required to deliver data to and from the core of the networks) and serve fewer revenue-generating customers due to lower population density. No wonder this population is among the hardest to connect, while being the most in need of that very connection.

▸ **Women**: In places like India and sub-Saharan Africa, women are 70% less likely than men to be connected. Not a recipe for dealing with the two-fold per-capita income gap between men and women globally or for addressing the troublingly unbalanced reality of two-thirds of illiterate adults in the world being women.

The connectivity challenge is a vicious circle: it is harder to increase your income if you're not connected, but it is harder to become connected if you cannot increase your income.

It takes an odd combination of near-term socialism, high-risk long-term capitalism and fast-moving commercial attitudes to break this stalemate. Governments, especially in countries most in need, rarely have the means to take significant steps; global telecommunications equipment providers like Cisco and Ericsson lack the financial strengths of days gone by to be involved deeply in the early and unprofitable days of bringing this "long tail" of people onto the Internet; and no telecommunications operator is global enough to influence the challenge beyond their local market, if they're even willing to go that far (although competition among local telecommunications operators is crucial to more affordable Internet access, as we can see from Kenya where competition among three large operators causes 21% of the population to be able to afford a 500-megabyte/month data plan, while in Ethiopia with a single operator almost no one can afford such a plan).

The list of global players who *can*—and *want to*—contribute to this challenge is short: Google and Facebook. Apple—holder of over $200 billion in cash and a key potential beneficiary of a more connected world—has appeared to be entirely absent.

Breaking Down the Problem the Zuckerberg Way

The economic, cultural, sociopolitical, educational, technical, regulatory and business issues of making headway in the connectivity challenge may appear overwhelming at first, second and even third glances, but just as one approaches the oversized task of eating the proverbial elephant one bite a time, so too Zuckerberg rationalized the giant undertaking—once it had entered the crosshairs of his and Facebook's mission—in three parts:

1. Availability: More than a billion people live entirely outside the coverage of today's mobile communications networks, largely due to the unattractive economics—higher-than-average cost and lower-than-average anticipated revenue—of supplying connectivity to these populations. As we saw in Chapter 5, Facebook's Connectivity Lab, under the engineering leadership of MIT PhD Yael Maguire, is not afraid to launch satellites (to cover sparse populations), build high-altitude UAVs with laser optics (for higher-density populations) and invent 10-fold efficiencies in urban terrestrial wireless technologies.

The aim in each case is for Facebook to take on the development risk for achieving cost breakthroughs and subsequently give away or license the technology to local infrastructure providers for them to address the unconnected or underserved—legacy 2G wireless infrastructure is as much a block to accessing the modern Internet as no infrastructure at all—with a better economic equation.

2. Affordability: Affecting another billion people, affordability of the Internet is less about the phone—the efficiencies of the scale of particularly the Google Android ecosystem are such that useful smartphones can be built to retail for well under $50 without subsidies by the telecommunication operators—and more about the cost of the data that, even for basic plans, can amount to two to three times the cost of the phone over its lifetime. Using less data (we've already seen how the low-bandwidth Facebook Lite has become Facebook's fastest product ever to 100 million users) and making data cheaper to deliver (the job of the Facebook-led open source Telecommunications Infrastructure Project) are the two gifts from Facebook to telecommunications operators on this front.

People in developing countries are already willing to spend twice the fraction of their income on data as are people in developed countries (3.8% vs. 1.8% on average and as divergent as 7% in Nigeria and 1% in the UK), but more reductions in the cost of infrastructure and competition between operators are necessary to meet people halfway on the road to broader connectivity.

But if everything comes together, progress can be made. The year 2014 showed that a 7% increase in income and a 12% decrease in the cost of data around the world can lead to an additional 500 million people globally being able to afford a 500-megabyte/month data plan.

3. Awareness and relevance: Who would have thought that one of the biggest parts of the connectivity challenge has nothing to do with technology and economics? It's difficult to imagine for those of us who open our phone over a hundred times a day to access the Internet, but in a survey of 42,000 people aged 15 to 64 in 11 countries across Latin America, Asia Pacific and Africa, 85% of the unconnected did not know what the Internet is, and half had never even heard the word.

Estimated by Facebook to be a blocker for as many as half of the 4 billion unconnected, the plan to address awareness and relevance of the Internet was to provide a simple and free on-ramp to a connected experience via stripped-down versions of Facebook's apps and other basic services, such as healthcare, education and job information compatible with local interests, cultures and needs, delivered by local providers bundled together in an application called Free Basics that telecommunications operators would offer for free to their mobile phone users who did not have a data plan. Led by Facebook's head of product partnerships—and former Yale basketball team captain—Ime Archibong and borne out of the 0.facebook.com service launched with selected telecommunications operators in May 2010, Free Basics launched in Zambia in July 2014 and by April 2016 had provided access to Facebook and 500 other services to 25 million people in 37 countries across the Middle East, Africa, Asia Pacific and Latin America. Half of the people who used Free Basics paid to access the Internet the following month.

Perhaps the only thing more surprising than awareness being such a sizable gap is that this seemingly less difficult to address aspect of the connectivity challenge would be the biggest stumbling block for Facebook in the early days.

Can't Give It Away

You'd think anything free would be easy to grow. Not so much.

To understand how Free Basics, a service that seems to provide nothing but upside for the underserved, could come first under scrutiny—and then fire—requires a little background on two complex and related issues: (1) net neutrality and (2) digital colonialism.

Net neutrality is the principle that no telecommunications operator should be allowed to throttle, differentially price or block access to any service on the Internet. Net neutrality's main job is to prevent an operator from fleecing you for the services that are important to you. You wouldn't want Verizon to charge you double your normal data rate for using your Facebook app or Comcast to charge you extra for each Google search. Conversely, net neutrality is also meant to avoid operators' advantaging certain services through lower data rates. It is this part of net neutrality that began to catch the attention of advocacy groups and some governments observing the so-called zero rating of Free Basics, a selection of services making up only a small part of the Internet—in a move considered misleading, the app was initially called internet.org—which were offered for free.

As for digital colonialism, the arrival of global connectivity has brought with it concerns over the emergence of digital versions of colonialist practices—the extension of control by one people from one territory to another possibly weaker and more dependent people and territory, a pattern most often associated with European overreach in the 16th to mid-20th centuries. Could a technology company deliver crucial capabilities to a particular part of the world that over time—whether by accident or design—undermine or control the choices and agency of those people. Incomplete Internet access? Misuse of personal information? Economic lock-in after "the first one was free"? Profiteering?

When you fan the budding flames of net neutrality concerns with the shades of digital colonialism that come with large multinational companies arriving with free gifts related to their commercial services that trade on people's information, perception problems can arise no matter how laudable the motive.

By May 2015, 65 advocacy groups from 31 countries expressed these misgivings in an open letter critical of Facebook, and several countries—including Egypt only five years after Facebook had played an enabling role in the Arab Spring—shut down Free Basics through regulatory means.

No criticism, however, was more withering—or impactful in perception and reality—than the January 2016 response by the Telecom Regulatory Authority of India (TRAI) to Facebook's awkward lobbying campaign—which had collected the commentary of over 10 million Indian Facebook users—for allowance of Free Basics in India, the single largest opportunity and need for the service with nearly 1 billion unconnected people. The regulatory body accused Facebook of "reducing this meaningful consultative exercise designed to produce informed decisions in a transparent manner into a crudely majoritarian and orchestrated opinion poll," suggested it would have "dangerous ramifications to policy-making in India" and expressed concern over Facebook's "self-appointed spokesmanship on behalf of those who have sent responses to TRAI using your platform." No wonder that the regulator blocked Free Basis the following month, a tough blow for the overall connectivity effort and for Zuckerberg who had written op-eds in *The Times of India* and appeared to enjoy a strong relationship with Indian Prime Minister Narendra Modi.

The day after the ban, Internet pioneer and Facebook board member Marc Andreessen appeared to give credence to the kind of digital colonialism fears—borne of India's experience with the likes of the East India Company, which at one point controlled half the world's trade and ruled the beginnings of the British Empire in India via private armies and the assumption of administrative functions—when in response to the ban he tweeted, "Anti-colonialism has been economically catastrophic for the Indian people for decades. Why stop now?" Zuckerberg strongly disavowed the comments the following day by saying that he found them "deeply upsetting, and they do not represent the way Facebook or I think at all" and that "to shape the future we need to understand the past . . . and I look forward to strengthening my connection to the country."

Clearly, finding on-ramps for the unconnected is a complex issue, as Zuckerberg is being doubted on one hand by shareholders concerned about the poor economics of the effort while simultaneously being vilified on the other hand by people who believe the move is grotesquely profit motivated.

Is the digital equivalent of small medical clinics and libraries that do not deliver access for everything and everyone but deliver what they can for free (an analogy first put forward by Andreessen Horowitz partner and former Microsoft President Steven Sinofsky) not better than no access for the poor and unconnected who have no voice in the online discourse on the topic? Is it impossible for those from Silicon Valley to appear anything but reductive in their arguments about connectivity challenges without understanding the complex local cultural, language and historical context? Is the pushback on Free Basics simply, as journalist David Kirkpatrick put it, "anti-corporate, anti-American and anti-poor"?

The Way Forward

As pitched as the battle over Free Basics appears to be (and not just in developing economies with *The Washington Post* reporting in October 2016 that Facebook is even working with the U.S. government to deliver Free Basics to low-income and rural Americans), it will not halt connectivity progress. At least two workable solutions present themselves:

Turn over the administration of Free Basics to neutral or even regulated bodies. This will align the perception of openness—one of the big concerns around Free Basics had been the fact that Facebook controls the effort and may gate access in ways deemed opaque or in direct conflict with popular opinion—with the already existing technical reality that Free Basics is an open platform with a published API and participation criteria that ensure the effective use of the technology. Facebook would continue to enable the effort via the technologies it develops, and telecommunications operators would use the service as a way to on-ramp previously unconnected users most able to evolve to paying for data plans, but local governments and populations would have the peace of mind that the on-ramp is not controlled by someone who may later exact a toll people do not want to pay.

Alternatively, Facebook could move beyond the Free Basics approach entirely and concentrate on ways to enable free on-ramps to the unfiltered Internet—and its popular Facebook Lite service—albeit with limits that make it economically feasible for operators to provide while still giving the previously unconnected an awareness of the Internet and its value. Novel tariffs—pay by the hour or day and limited-time free samplers during low-utilization hours—create low-risk opportunities for operators to create awareness while appreciating the crushing daily economic uncertainty of the unconnected who live close to and below the poverty line. Journalist, entrepreneur and cofounder of SaveTheInternet.in Nikhil Pahwa, writing in *The Times of India*, perhaps captured the sentiment of this approach best: "The trade-off users are willing to make is how much they use the Internet, not necessarily how much of the Internet they get to use."

Either way, Facebook will continue to focus on doing the unprofitable heavy lifting of developing hardware and software—from satellites and drones to network architectures and services obsessed with the efficient use of scarce bandwidth, like Facebook Lite—in order to show that higher scale *and* lower cost are feasible and then partner with or give away the technology to players that have the local experience and long-term business incentive to make these technologies thrive with the next few billion people.

The circumstances in Facebook's efforts to connect the unconnected are just another example of the Facebook way and therefore the Zuckerberg way: not everything will work at first—or even be conceived in the best possible way—but it is better to act and adjust than to wait, and Zuckerberg and his teams have just enough humility neither to be put off by failure nor to resist changing their approach after new learnings. It's the only way Facebook knows. It is the way that has gotten them as far as they have. And they will not stop now.

15

"Transporting" a Billion of Us with VR and AR

Building the last screen

As I was walking through the Facebook offices on March 25, 2014, a friend stopped me in surprise to read me the announcement of Facebook's $2 billion acquisition of little-known virtual reality (VR) headset maker Oculus VR.

As a confessed tech-headline-of-the-day hunter, I was aware of Oculus's crowd-funded indie project to put screens and head tracking sensors into what looked like heavy—and heavily duct-taped—ski goggles with an elaborate umbilical cord back to a kind of souped-up, blinking mini fridge computer that serious gamers kept under their desk the way street racers keep their perfectly waxed Japanese-made tuners in their garage.

Nevertheless, coming just a month after the $19 billion WhatsApp blockbuster had marked Facebook's 40th acquisition, I wondered for a moment whether my friend had read me a headline from satirical news website *The Onion* mocking Facebook's acquisitive streak.

How did Oculus VR fit with Facebook?

Shortly after the acquisition news had hit the public relations wire, Zuckerberg took to Facebook to address *that* question by asking—and answering—a question of his own:

> What platforms will come next to enable even more useful, entertaining and personal experiences?
>
> . . .

> Oculus' mission is to enable you to experience the impossi-
> ble. Their technology opens up the possibility of completely
> new kinds of experiences.
>
> . . .
>
> Imagine enjoying a court side seat at a game, studying in a
> classroom of students and teachers all over the world or
> consulting with a doctor face-to-face—just by putting on
> goggles in your home.
>
> . . .
>
> One day, we believe this kind of immersive, augmented real-
> ity will become a part of daily life for billions of people.

It slowly became clear that this was just crazy enough to work. But, to believe that, you have to zoom out. A lot.

The roughly 70-year history of computing makes it undeniably clear
that no platform or interface lasts in a specific state forever. Room-sized
mainframe computers of the 1950s and 1960s were overtaken by cabinet-
sized minicomputers in the 1970s, which were overtaken by desktop and
laptop PCs in the 1980s and 1990s, which themselves were overtaken—in
the largest and fastest disruption ever—by smartphones in the 2010s.
As well documented as this long pattern of disruption is, it can still catch
leaders of one era by surprise. You can see in Figure 15-1 how hard it is to
be paranoid during a particular platform's salad days: the PC industry's
projections in 2004 of PCs (the upper dashed line) and smartphones (the
lower dashed line) sales over the coming decade were completely upset
just a half dozen years later.

This lesson is not lost on Zuckerberg. No matter how crucial the emergence of mobile—and Zuckerberg's famous internal I'll-end-the-meeting-
if-you-don't-show-me-a-mobile-screenshot-of-your-product-first
push—was to Facebook's unrivaled worldwide leadership in user engagement, he can't assume that mobile in its current form will be the dominant
medium in five to 10 years.

The time for the watchful CEO to look ahead was five minutes ago because perhaps the only thing better than being mobile is being "transported" by VR and its more-likely-to-succeed-at-global-scale cousin,
Augmented Reality (AR).

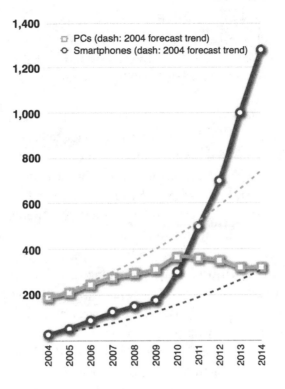

Figure 15-1. Global sales of PCs and smartphones (millions)

How Can VR and AR Possibly Matter to You and Facebook?

We'll get to the motley crew at Oculus working to make all this possible in a minute. They include the 23-year-old undergrad dropout you might expect, the 59-year-old PhD dropout you wouldn't, a revered gaming wizard and the new Pixar made up of the old Pixar. Some of them have been waiting more than 25 years for technology to catch up to their vision and that of *Star Trek*'s holodeck, Neal Stephenson's *Snowcrash*, Morpheus and Neo in *The Matrix* and Ernest Cline's *Ready Player One*.

But first, why do virtual reality and augmented reality matter?

If you have technology that can track head movement, recompute 60 to 90 times a second what you should see corresponding to that new position from two slightly horizontally separated viewpoints simulating your eyes and display the two results on high-resolution screens mere inches from your eyes enclosed in a head-mounted display (HMD) such that they are all you see, and if it can do all of that in 20 to 30 milliseconds, you can fool a person's vision and brain into believing that they "are" somewhere "else," possibly "with" others. A feeling known as "presence."

Reality, therefore, is merely what your brain believes it is.

Once you expand what someone can be made to believe through VR, you can build games that give you fantastical powers in impossible places. Watch your friends' Italian vacation videos in their full 360-degree 3D splendor. Watch an NBA game as if you were courtside. Sit in the front row of a college lecture by a world-class expert even though you live in a small town halfway around the world. Be *in* a movie rather than watch it. Develop life-changing empathy to the conditions in a refugee camp without having actually visited it, perhaps making virtual reality as a medium to human suffering and inequality what video was to war whether as newsreel (World War II), broadcast (Vietnam) or gun camera (Desert Storm). Talk and work with people thousands of miles away in ways as immediate as if they were in the same room. Pull that junior high school classroom into medieval times to depths for which you would have previously needed a Michael Crichton best seller. Train athletes, doctors, pilots and soldiers in ways that are both more visceral *and* safer. Even use exposure therapy to help the majority of us that suffer from fears to overcome them.

A technology slightly less heady than VR but perhaps even more useful in the long term is augmented reality (AR), which shares many of the technical requirements but seeks to overlay visual information on your existing world rather than to replace that world entirely. It comes in the general form of glasses with clear lenses onto which the visuals are rendered. The visuals can be something as simple as the text of a message displayed in a corner of your glasses or as sophisticated as information related to something or someone in your field of view where the visuals are constantly re-rendered to match the location of that target in your actual view.

Once you can combine generated visuals with your actual world, you can do navigation for driving and walking the way it always should have been: right onto the path in front of you. Virtually annotate the people and things at live sporting events, concerts, theater productions and museum exhibits. Translate what you are seeing and hearing in real time. Play a game of *Settlers of Catan*—or *Star Wars* Dejarik holochess—on the empty table in front of you with your friend from Minneapolis. Extend what you are seeing on television to your family room. Work on six virtual displays on your desk instead of the 13-inch screen on your laptop. Or just watch Netflix on a virtual 120-inch TV instead of the actual 45-inch one hanging on your wall.

VR and AR are not just the *next* screens. They are the first screens with no edges, and, as screens capable of simulating all other screens, they are our *last* screens. As unlikely or even as fantastical as this may sound if you have not experienced it, VR and AR are just another step forward in the multimillennial progress of human media: from language to typography to pictures to video to ... experiences.

And that is why they matter to Facebook. As a means to drive forward the mission to make the world more open and connected. To connect more viscerally, empathize more deeply and be transported more completely.

That, however, is not the *whole* truth. As much as VR and AR create possibilities for user experiences far beyond merely showing you Facebook's News Feed on your glasses, there is one other big reason that they matter to Zuckerberg: strategic protection against being disrupted in a media transition occurring over the next five to 10 years, which in the complicated world of technology could come from below, beside or above Facebook.

Most important in the category of competitors *below* Facebook are the operating systems on which the service runs—especially Apple's iOS and Google's Android. Even today, these operating systems—which require developers of apps to exist in a controlled environment accessible only by going through Apple's and Google's approval process to be made available in their respective app stores—exert a tremendous amount of control that is Zuckerberg's greatest strategic concern. Luckily, the current situation is one of mutually assured destruction as neither operating system would use its strategic choke point to block Facebook, their most heavily used app. However, if a transition to a new or evolved medium like VR and AR would allow either Apple or Google to prevent or disadvantage Facebook from evolving, things could erode quickly.

Competition *beside* Facebook would be another "lens" (recall Chapter

4) emerging to play a bigger role in people's ability to connect with the world. Google is Facebook's biggest competitor here, and if they could advance an interesting technology—or perspective on the world—using VR and AR faster than Facebook, they would threaten the stranglehold Zuckerberg has on people's attention as their lens on the world.

And competition from *above* would come in the form of interesting future content and experiences—especially around VR and AR—that people want to connect with and that Facebook did not have access to or that could not be shared via Facebook. People's attention, like water, will find a way around the obstacles of the no-longer-cool to the most interesting things.

Having the hardware, software and content efforts of Oculus—and VR and AR generally—running early in this perhaps decade-long window of strategic uncertainty gives Facebook the best possible experience, tools and bargaining chips to adjust to the realities of a significant transition if and when it occurs.

Who Are These People?

Oculus VR—which along with artificial intelligence is one of Zuckerberg's most important bets for the foundation of Facebook's future—started in 2011 with Palmer Luckey, a then 18-year-old homeschooled tinkerer from Long Beach, California. Luckey's hobby of repairing smartphones threw off enough money and the kind of miniaturized electrical components necessary that he was able to turn his interest in VR headsets—he had collected more than 50 examples of the species—into building an HMD of his own.

VR HMDs have a long history of being bedeviled by technical issues that prevent a true feeling of immersion: screen resolution, width of the field of view (FOV), smearing visuals of displays with persistence delays between successive images and especially the time it takes between head movement and corresponding screen refresh, known more technically as motion-to-photon latency, that can cause discomfort when the brain experiences dissonance between movement and vision. Luckey, however—benefiting from the advances in screens and sensors that former *Wired* editor Chris Anderson has called "the peace dividend of the smartphone wars"—was starting to make real progress.

As is often the case in the infinite bazaar of ideas that is the Internet, Palmer's progress attracted attention.

One of the people taking note in the summer of 2012 was pixel wizard John Carmack. Widely considered the most important and broadly influential graphics and gaming coder of the prior two decades, Carmack—42 at the time—was credited on over 40 games, including the seminal *Castle Wolfenstein*, *Doom* and *Quake* franchises and more than half a dozen groundbreaking graphics engines used by countless other games. His career at id software, the gaming company he founded, was the thing of legends. As the high priest of how to turn zeroes and ones into images that immerse you, Carmack could enthrall the masses at id's conventions for three-and-a-half-hour keynotes. Even Steve Jobs' keynote superpowers topped out at around two hours.

According to Carmack's own recollections, the psychological evaluation he was ordered to undertake after being arrested for computer theft at the age of 14 and prior to serving a year in a juvenile home diagnosed him as a "brain on legs."

It should come as no surprise, then, that after more than two decades of programming and 2 million lines of graphics code, the untiring Carmack began to tinker with VR headsets in June and July of 2012 on his own. However, upon asking Luckey for a prototype of the Oculus Rift—and promptly receiving from him the only working one—Carmack became a convert to the headset just ahead of the E3 gaming show in Los Angeles in August.

Another convert at that time was gaming industry veteran Brendan Iribe. The then 32-year-old was coming off stints as a user interface programmer on the strategy gaming franchise *Civilization*, as cofounder of a user interface technology provider that had been sold to Autodesk, and as product team lead at a streaming gaming provider that had just been acquired in July 2012 by Sony for its PlayStation franchise.

Casting about, Iribe's keen eye for the visual future of computing caught Luckey's ever growing Oculus Rift campfire, and Iribe would come aboard as Oculus's CEO just ahead of the crowd-funding campaign that would change the course of VR.

Following the wildly successful Kickstarter campaign in August of 2012 that had aimed to secure $250,000 from backers but wound up receiving $2.4 million in the first 24 hours alone, and delivering the first Oculus Rift Developer Kit headset (DK1) in March of 2013, John Carmack would formally end his 22-year career at id software to become CTO of Oculus in August of 2013. Saying that the feeling of "presence is religion on contact," Carmack was ready to start the next chapter of his prolific career.

In March 2014, in a scene mirroring conversations with Kevin Systrom over Instagram and Jan Koum over WhatsApp, Iribe struck the $2 billion deal to be acquired by Facebook one-on-one at Zuckerberg's house.

Only a few days later, Oculus would announce the arrival of the final puzzle piece in their technical team as computer graphics and VR veteran Michael Abrash joined as chief scientist. The then-57-year-old Abrash was a respected programmer with stints at Microsoft's operating system, natural language processing (NLP) research and XBOX divisions, id (where he had worked with Carmack), gaming tools developer RAD, Intel and game developer Valve. More importantly, he was also an expert on the human perceptual system and a VR philosopher. It is Abrash who most often makes poetic pronouncements like, "If the world wide web was alpha, then VR is omega."

Between Luckey, Carmack and Abrash, Oculus VR has an outsized share of the best pixel pushers in the world, but they haven't stopped there. To make sure that Oculus is also a leader in the actual pixels that are being pushed, they formed Oculus Story Studio in August 2014, a combination of lab and production studio meant to discover and openly share with the industry how to move various media forward into the rich—but poorly explored—opportunities of VR and AR.

Oculus Story Studio is a Pixar for VR. Fittingly, it is led and comprised of many former Pixar employees.

Oculus Story Studio Creative Director Saschka Unseld was at Pixar for six years, including as director of the short film *Blue Umbrella*; Technical

Director Max Planck was at Pixar for a decade and worked on half a dozen of their feature films; and Director Ramiro Lopez Dau was at Pixar for five years and worked on three films. All in all, as of spring 2016, a third of Oculus Story Studio's 30 employees had stints at Pixar in their backgrounds. Their first three VR "films," *Lost*, *Henry* and *Dear Angelica*, featured a missing robot hand finding its owner, a lonely hedgehog who likes hugs and balloons, and a daughter going through her mother's memories in the form of 3D impressionistic illustrations.

All these efforts would culminate—nearly five year's after Palmer Luckey's first prototype—in the launch of Oculus VR's first consumer version of the Rift headset (CV1) in March 2016. A successor is already planned for 2018 or 2019.

How We Go from Ski Goggles to a Billion Users

Virtual and augmented reality are powerful magic, so the current push is not the first time the industry has tried their hand at it. First efforts on VR HMDs came from graphics pioneer Ivan Sutherland in the late 1960s and were revived in the mid-1980s by Jaron Lanier and his company VPL Research, whose HMD was called—no kidding—Eye Phone. Cultural figures no less important than Timothy Leary would partake in the technology, but the demands of making your brain truly believe in an alternate reality exceeded what was technically possible in the past.

But, as of 2016, we're finally at a point to take VR and AR to consumer scale, and Facebook is certainly not the only one working on it.

With all six of the largest consumer technology companies in the world deeply invested and feverishly in development, VR and AR have become too big to fail.

Oculus Rift, Samsung GearVR (powered by Oculus), Google Cardboard and Google's Magic Leap investment (and perhaps even the second coming of Google Glass), Sony PlayStation VR and Microsoft HoloLens are already public, and the eventual entry of Apple is presumed, given hiring headlines and CEO Tim Cook's pronouncement that VR and AR are not a niche application.

However, as much as 2016 saw the launches of the best VR to date with Oculus Rift, HTC Vive and PlayStation VR, this generation of hardware—not portable and tethered to a PC or gaming console—is merely intended for millions of early adopter enthusiasts consisting mostly of gamers. HMDs of 2016 are to the future of VR and AR what Gordon Gecko's brick-like Motorola cellular phone is to your rose-gold iPhone 7.

The devices that *will* turn VR and AR into an interface for hundreds of millions will blend into our lives much more easily. To do that, they will embrace the one device that rules them all—the smartphone—and in doing so pull it out of its stagnation.

They will look and feel much like ordinary large-framed glasses and feature clear lenses with built-in waveguides transmitting the output of tiny projectors on each arm across the entire surface of each lens, covering a total 120-degree field of view with 90-frame/second, 1,080p video (960 × 1080 resolution for each eye) that will be delivered wirelessly by your phone. In the out years it's even possible the projection-plus-waveguide combination will be replaced with extremely high-resolution transparent edge-to-edge LCDs in each lens.

Instead of distinguishing between AR and VR, these glasses will have the ability to go from being completely clear (off) to displaying images that augment what you see (AR) to displaying images that cover the lenses edge to edge (VR), leveraging next-generation phones for all the computing necessary. While they will sacrifice some of the image quality and perfect sense of virtual reality "presence" that large, fully enclosed HMDs tethered to PCs can deliver, they will suffice for the vast majority of popular VR and AR applications and be dramatically easier to wear and carry, driving much greater consumer adoption than more complex HMDs, which will stick around to serve the high-end gaming community.

While the performance and miniaturization demanded by this lightweight alternative are not available at consumer scale in 2016, prototypes of the necessary technologies exist, making the first easy-to-wear, consumer-grade VR/AR glasses plausible between 2018 and 2020.

With this approach, the glasses benefit from the popularity, portability, connectivity, computing, touch and voice controls that the phone can deliver, and the phone benefits from the new display options and applications the glasses make possible.

Instead of an entirely new and different platform, these VR/AR glasses will be an evolution and extension of mobile.

Looking at the major players for mainstream VR/AR glasses, I would project another competition between Apple (starting in the form of Apple Glasses 1 together with a new iPhone between 2018 and 2020) and a federation of hardware suppliers—including Samsung and Facebook's Oculus—on a Google platform connected to Android. On the services and content front, expect Facebook to evolve all its offerings—Facebook, Instagram, Messenger, WhatsApp and potential new additions—to take advantage of the capabilities that AR and VR offer and to make them available for both Apple and Google hardware platforms as they do today. Expect Facebook also to have to wrestle with uncomfortable questions about the topic of pornography in VR and AR. Facebook and Instagram have always had policies preventing such content, and, similar to Apple's App Store and Google Play, the Oculus VR and Samsung GearVR stores will not allow adult entertainment either, but unlike the Apple iPhone and Google Android phone, Oculus VR is open to all developers, and pornography is rapidly finding its way onto the platform.

How big can the extension of the mobile medium to VR and AR get? Looking at the market for tablets that began in earnest in 2010 with the introduction of the Apple iPad may be instructive as an upper bound for projections since prices—anywhere from $300 to $800—and use cases are similar:

▸ Since its introduction in 2010, nearly 300 million Apple iPads have been sold.

▸ Total annual tablet sales are predicted to be 300 million by 2018.

▸ An installed base of about 1 billion is expected by 2018.

Keeping in mind that VR/AR glasses will be a newer medium in 2018 than tablets were in 2010 and that glasses may not drop to low-end price points as rapidly as the more familiar tablet technologies, it may be difficult for glasses to get all the way to an installed base of 1 billion by 2026—eight years after their mainstreaming in 2018. But an installed base above 500 million by 2026 is plausible, and as our "last screen," the glasses are likely to continue to build momentum to an installed base of 1 billion, especially as the smartphones powering the glasses are expected to go to a total installed base in excess of 5 billion in that time frame.

Transporting a billion of us is no less likely than connecting a billion of us to begin with.

16

What If Facebook "Wins"?

Reknitting the Pangea of the mind

With a mission as big as Facebook's, a constant refrain—at least internally—that Facebook's "journey is only 1% done" and with all of us heads-down in our phones, we don't think much about what happens if Facebook—for lack of a better word—"wins."
If they serve a Facebook-sized share of China's Internet population. If they connect the unconnected, especially in India and Africa, with drones and satellites. If they make video—all our phones will have 3D 360-degree video by 2025—as ubiquitous as photos are today. If you can feel as though you can "be" nearly anywhere nearly anytime and discover and watch all of it—including commercial television—right in what Facebook's pervasive News Feed will come to be on our lightweight mixed-reality glasses connected wirelessly to our phones. If we have an extra half hour a day for these perfectly bite-sized services because our self-driving cars are taking care of our commute. If Facebook turns their youngest assets—WhatsApp and Messenger—into their most popular tools, spreading easy-to-use messaging-based services far beyond WeChat's and Line's beginnings in Asia. If we search less and know more because Facebook underpins all their services with artificial intelligence that—truly—knows, understands and anticipates each of us.

That would be big, but roughly how big?

Hypothetically: Facebook 2025

By 2025, world population is estimated to be 8.1 billion people.[1] Combining projections[2] and some conservative trend analysis, the Internet population could grow to 5 billion people by that time. If Facebook's services were to have a 60% penetration of that entire Internet population (well below their average penetration in 2015 in the dozens of countries that don't have fundamental connectivity issues or competitive challenges) **the company would be serving 3 billion people and well over 100 million businesses a month.**

That would be much more significant than merely "twice its size in 2015." Since the value of a telecommunications network grows with the square of its size (thank you, Metcalfe's law), Facebook's services would be four times more aware because of all the extra eyes and minds and four times more productive because of the increase in economic participants. It wouldn't just be nearly twice its current share of the world's total population (up from 20% to 37%) because, assuming that Facebook penetrates an average of 50% of each cohort in the distribution of the world's population (a crude estimate), a 37% total share could perhaps reach down to the 26th economic, educational, health and infrastructure percentile of the world's population instead of merely the 60th. Those are populations with a 10- to 100-fold difference in means.

While still just a partial reflection of society and the globe, it would be *very* big.

But forget about size. Is there a chance that Facebook could be "more" than just more? Something beyond just bigger, faster and whizzier?

How 2005 May Have Been Like 1493: The Columbian Exchange of the Mind

What happens when we sail to the edge of the online world? Could it usher in a postconnectivity era? Could Zuckerberg become the Columbus of the Mind, Facebook its Columbian Exchange, and in doing so reknit the Pangea of society?

Say what?

To make sense of that last sentence, I need to back up. To 1493. Or, more accurately, to *1493*.[3] In his 2011 best seller, Charles Mann describes the profound impact that Columbus's voyages had—even if largely unwittingly—on connecting the previously disparate Europe, Africa, Asia and Americas and triggering the globalization that defines the world today.

Fundamental to this was the so-called Columbian Exchange (a concept first introduced by Alfred Crosby[4] in 1972) that brought goods, animals, food—and disease—from one corner of the world and established and redistributed them to many others. The Columbian Exchange, as Mann puts it, "is the reason there are tomatoes in Italy, oranges in the US, chocolate in Switzerland and chilis in Thailand." It brought horses from Europe, earthworms crucial for agriculture from South America to North America where they had been frozen out by the Ice Age, silver from South America—mined by African slaves under the thumb of Europeans—to Asia, in return for the silk and porcelain prized by the Europeans, fertilizer based on Guano from Peru, sugarcane from New Guinea, wheat from the Middle East, rubber from Brazil, tobacco from the Caribbean and coffee from Africa. It was responsible for gigantic biological crises like introducing smallpox, measles, typhoid fever, cholera and malaria to the Americas and syphilis and the potato famine to Europe. It underlies, in Mann's assessment, the Industrial Revolution, the Agricultural Revolution and the rise of the West.

The abstract notion of the Columbian Exchange is perhaps the single greatest influence on shaping life in the physical world in the last 500 years, a process Crosby called "the re-knitting of Pangea" in reference to Earth's single land mass that began to break apart about 175 million years ago.

With that in mind, could Facebook with 3 billion users be the Columbian Exchange of the mind and Zuckerberg its catalyst (a comparison that doesn't necessarily do Zuckerberg any favors considering Columbus's detractors over issues such as slavery, direct and indirect genocide, poor navigation and religious fanaticism)?

There are some very strong parallels between Facebook—especially at 3 billion users—and the Columbian Exchange in that they both enable connections on a new platform. As Spaniards traveled to Mexico in the early 16th century and then sailed to the Philippines, where they met Chinese traders, so too do we connect with friends half a world away via Facebook.

But there remains a big gap. While Facebook charts hundreds of billions of human connections, it is much less *diverse* an "exchange" than its Columbian counterpart. Unlike that first meeting between the Spaniards and the Chinese in the Philippines that initiated the so-called galleon trade, our feelings, stories and ideas—the goods of the heart and mind—don't flow between *new* connections nearly as much on Facebook's services. We may be *from* the global community, but we haven't *formed* a global community. We are overwhelmingly connected to people and things we already knew, and our News Feed works to show us more of who and what we've Like'd before. It trends—for better or worse—to being an echo chamber rather than an exchange. At its weakest, it is institutionalized confirmation bias, the tendency to seek out, interpret, prefer and remember information closer to our own opinions, causing us to grow more entrenched in them.

Imagine . . .

The very things that create that echo chamber, Facebook's recommended connections and its News Feed, also have the power to go far beyond it: to take "the great left-hand turn" and, in addition to connecting us to whom and what we *know*, become dramatically more active in connecting us to whom and what we do *not*. To connect you not just with "your" world but "the" world. To the other side not just of the planet but of issues. Not just to amazon.com but to Banana Boat in Uganda and Dhatu Rembulan in Indonesia. To not just enhance existing connections but to rewire them and even introduce entirely new ones. To see if in some small—or large—measure, our *online* community can break out of the balkanization of our *physical* one.

What if we can find a way to help Republicans better understand the positions that are causing support for Democrats (and vice versa), for Americans who have been unable to make meaningful progress on gun control to hear more from Australians who have, for men to connect more easily with women working to overcome unconscious biases in the workplace, for traditional families to build more empathy for modern families, for the white suburbanite to better understand why #blacklivesmatter shouldn't be called #alllivesmatter, for a Silicon Valley techie to hear from their user in Iowa, for an Iraqi Muslim mother and a Texas Christian mother to exchange pictures of their daughters. For a top African developer to have the chance to work with a Fortune 500 company or startup (which happens to be the mission of the Chan Zuckerberg Initiative's first $24 million investment, Nigerian technology firm Andela).

What would that take? Well, for starters, a *lot* of people (check). An understanding of how those people are connected (check). A lot of data, content and points of view flowing between connections (check). The ability to easily surface new connections (check) and to share content and messages (check). The artificial intelligence necessary to effectively translate the written and spoken word between dozens of languages (in 2016 Facebook launched automatic text translations for 44 languages, so check) and perhaps even the ability to create intelligent bots that act like other people and points of view in the world (check).

How would it work? To find out, I asked my daughter, a young Millennial (or old Generation Z, depending on which demographer you ask). After thinking about how to slowly broaden perspectives without jumping into the deep end of the pool of better mutual global understanding by dumping you into a chat with strangers who have different points of view from yours, live in places you've never been or know things that you don't understand, she suggested repurposing a Facebook feature you already see many times a day.

After you click on a link in your News Feed, Facebook uses your expressed interest to show a collection of Related Links similar to the content you just viewed. With Facebook's advancing artificial intelligence increasingly able to go from merely matching words to understanding meaning—and therefore also more relationships more complicated than "similar," such as "deeper," "different" and "opposing"—it could do more than just show you similar links, reserving room to also show you links from expanded and different perspectives, including translated versions of views from other countries. You'd be free to ignore these links, but the opportunity to broaden your horizons will tempt you at every turn.

Once the ball starts rolling, you continue to leverage the AI's ability to deduce meaning by extending the "balanced perspective" feature to friends and businesses' status updates ("We noticed you liked your friend's post about gun control. Would you like to explore additional perspectives?" "You clicked on home furnishings at Target. Would you also like to shop Skinny laMinx in Cape Town, South Africa?").

Then you take the big step of offering people dialog to expand their views. But, instead of connecting you with a person—which may feel awkward—Facebook will be able to offer you an intermediate step: connecting you with a bot that has learned about certain perspectives from Facebook's aggregated data. With a significant amount of the aggregated "consciousness" (Likes, status updates, shared links, images, video) of 3 billion people available to learn from—and Facebook would be the only ones with this asset—Facebook of 2025 could offer you a Republican bot *and* a Democratic bot. A bot that loves the Red Sox *and* a bot that loves the Yankees. A bot that can converse about life in Ghana. A bot that can talk to you about the tensions between India and Pakistan, reflecting both perspectives.

Go ahead, ask a bot, "Why are you Republican?" or "How do Palestinians feel the conflict with Israel could be de-escalated?" or "Is Tom Brady really the greatest of all time?" Bots don't judge, won't make fun of you to their friends and can't get their feelings hurt, and you'll be one answer more informed after your chat.

And, finally, when people are not just comfortable with occasionally looking for a more complete perspective but feel better for having done so, you can create ways of making communication connections with other real people. To ease the process, you allow anonymous connection requests over specific topics where identities are revealed only with mutual consent. "A person from Syria would like to talk to someone in Germany about the refugee situation. Are you willing to chat anonymously?" "A person from the United States would like to talk to someone in Iraq about fundamentalist Islam. Are you willing to chat anonymously?" "A full-stack mobile app developer from Pakistan with a 4.8/5.0 rating would like to connect with China-based mobile game developers. Are you willing to chat anonymously?" "A maker of artisanal pasta sauces in Sienna Italy with a 4.9/5 rating would like to connect with people in the United States who like pasta or have been to Italian restaurants in the last month. Are you willing to chat anonymously?" Think of it as Tinder's "swiping right" for what Cuban anthropologist Fernando Ortiz called "transculturation."

Nice vision, but you're asking yourself why people would participate in this exchange to broaden their perspective when for millennia they've shown the tendency to do the exact opposite.

For the original Columbian Exchange, the primary motivations for the incredible depth and breadth of participation were its commerce opportunities and the better lives—and greater power—they promised to bring to all involved (although it turns out the Exchange rebalanced economic power from Asia to Europe and the Americas, a crucial tipping point in their subsequent rise). While there are shades of this kind of economic opportunity in a more diversely connected Facebook 2025, they would affect merely a few hundred million people, not billions.

But, never underestimate the power of prestige (or, at least, self-curation and psychic income, the subjective benefits beyond financial gain that make us feel good). A major force of the Columbian Exchange's early days and the reason Columbus enjoyed tremendous support from Spain's government upon returning from his first voyage was Europe's desire to trade silver from South America with Asia to obtain silk and porcelain, which lack—at least relatively—the financial value to their eventual owner of a horse, new land or exotic seeds. They did, however, make you feel better.

Maybe, just maybe, there is a trace of those feel-good chemicals to be had in Facebook 2025. And few things are more powerful in bringing them to the surface than a visible number or two. Not sure what I mean? How many people liked that picture you posted earlier?

What if Facebook added a new Reaction or two (beyond Like, Love, HaHa, Wow, Sad, Angry): "Andrea *discovered* a post by Exodus: Our Journey to Europe." "Steve *heard* Robert's post." Or introduced a new kind of connection: "Maria made a World Connection with Anja in Croatia." "David has 440 Friends and 26 World Connections." The all-powerful News Feed algorithm—Zuckerberg's equivalent of Adam Smith's "invisible hand"—will prefer to surface stories of these reactions and connections, and we know what happens when Facebook can get an active minority engaged with a feature. We do what our friends do, even if that is making new kinds of friends.

Put a Growth Team on that, and we may be on our way to something much bigger than just 3 billion people: reknitting the Pangea of the mind.

4

Parting Thoughts

17

Failure Isn't

***Facebook doesn't always hit it out of the park,
and that's a good thing***

An appetite for wildly irrational levels of risk and celebration of failure are two of the most central aspects of Silicon Valley and its lore.
This is not a place for the timid. It is, instead, a crucible of creative destruction. New dreams are built—literally—on top of old ones that failed
to keep up. Just see Google's campus at the site of the now defunct graphics workstation maker SGI and Facebook's constantly expanding campus
on the site of acquired-and-forgotten-former "dot in dotcom" SUN.

A lack of fear of failure is what has changed Silicon Valley itself to no
longer revolve primarily around its namesake "Silicon" and practically
ensures that it will continue to evolve to meet the needs and opportunities of the future the same way it has since its origin among fruit orchards
in the 1950s.

Striking out forward with no certainty of outcome is Silicon Valley's
reason for being.

Risk is required and failure inherent, but the two have to be managed
differently by the valley's two primary types of consumer businesses.

Hardware makers like Apple and even Tesla have to tread more cau-
tiously. Cycle times to build new product categories—and/or recover from
mistakes in previous products—are long, investments in the large teams
and complex manufacturing required are high and expectations from paying consumers unforgiving. You inherently get fewer at-bats and are forced
to swing in a considered way to clear the fences as often as possible.

Software, on the other hand, now almost exclusively in the form of
free-to-use Internet-based services like Google and Facebook, cannot
afford to act with anything but wild abandon. Risks are comparatively

negligible—prototypes can be built quickly with small teams and little variable costs—making competition, even from smaller players, rampant and disruption a reality around every corner. As Zuckerberg said in 2011, "In a world that is changing really quickly, the only strategy that is guaranteed to fail is not taking risks."

That's why it feels like Google and Facebook are constantly throwing things against the wall to see what sticks, while Apple takes three to five years to build their first devices in a new category, and Tesla will arrive at their $35,000 Model 3 after a 10-year journey.

In this competitive soup, Facebook is certainly not the first to embrace failure but has become one of the best.

Hacking Failure

At Facebook, failure doesn't just happen. Risk and failure are *institutionalized* as opposed to merely allowed or encouraged.

Risk and failure live in its culture, made real through the hundreds of posters that dot nearly every available vertical space on campus—"What would you do if you weren't afraid?" "Move fast and break things" "Fail harder" "Think wrong"—and the actions of *all* the people around you, not just the culture-carrying veterans.

They live in one of Facebook's most celebrated practices: Hackathons. Multiple times a year, the company—especially engineering but increasingly other functions as well—comes to a stop and, for a 24-hour period, works on building prototypes in very small groups formed around passion projects that otherwise would not be able to receive time and attention. Important to closing the loop on this cultural touchstone is that Zuckerberg himself reviews the best projects, and a few are subsequently greenlighted to be developed into real products. Some Hackathon projects—like tagging people in photos, the ability to post videos and the game-changing performance benefits to Facebook infrastructure of HipHop for PHP—succeed wildly, while others—like Snapchat "homage" Slingshot—do not, but all efforts and outcomes are celebrated.

And they live, most importantly, in Zuckerberg himself—who shows it in big ways, such as the acquisitions of Instagram, WhatsApp and Oculus VR and moonshot projects like the Connectivity Lab and Artificial Intelligence Research, and in small ways like his personal project in 2016 to build a Messenger bot to control his own home and ownership of his leadership failures—that, like everything else at Facebook and to a greater extent than any other public company CEO, an appetite for risk and failure starts with him.

Good thing, because there's been a lot of both. Whether additions to Facebook's main service, products for advertisers, acquisitions or entirely new apps, many a Facebook swing has been a miss.

"Failures": The Big Blue App

Although they become harder to remember with every headline of another hundred million people using Facebook's main service on a daily basis, the company's central effort has not escaped its share of unfulfilled dreams.

In the earlier days, the internal enthusiasm around **Virtual Gifts** (from February 2007 to July 2010) and **Questions** (July 2010 to October 2012) to drive greater structure and engagement around two popular activities between people on Facebook—birthday wishes and learning from the "hive mind" of your friends and friends of friends—was met with some uptake by the community, but it did not spread to wide and regular use, the bar for which, at Facebook, hovers in the hundreds of millions of monthly users. Interestingly, the two suffered from opposite issues as Virtual Gifts was simply not used by a broad enough set of people to "role-model" the behavior—we do what our friends do—while Questions suffered from too many seeming nonexperts weighing in on the queries posted by friends, making the corresponding outcomes seem less curated than the smaller but more successful community at Quora, a service dedicated to the premise and cofounded by former Facebooker Adam D'Angelo.

Two misses more central to the business followed with the all-hands-on-deck construction and almost equally fast shutdown of **Deals** (April 2011 to August 2011), a way to buy and share coupons for goods and services from businesses directly in News Feed, and the awkwardly named **Graph Search** (March 2013 to December 2014), a vision of search constructed specifically for Facebook's giant collection of people, photos, connections, Pages, Places and content. Deals, an attempt to respond to the seemingly meteoric success of coupons-reinvented-for-the-Internet purveyor Groupon, suffered from issues inherent to the category, as special group deals proved faddish and unsustainable by the entire sector but most especially by the small and medium-sized businesses they were supposed to grow. They have since been replaced by more effective and consistent ways to raise awareness and purchase for businesses and products over the longer term, including Offers, in-line Buy buttons and the ability to relate Facebook marketing activity to in-store footfall. Graph Search, a highly structured semantic search of Facebook (e.g., "friends of Jane Doe who like Beyoncé and Vin Diesel," "my friends who work at Apple," "my friends from Europe who have visited Italy," "pictures of me and John Doe") was sophisticated but difficult-to-use and did not substantially grow the use of Facebook search beyond looking for people. Since that project, a focus on searching status updates and comments for keywords has been more pragmatic and successful, but more is possible, and necessary, for Facebook.

"Failures": Advertising

Facebook has built the preeminent mobile advertising product in the world, but the road to that product has on occasion been bumpy.

In its early days, Facebook misstepped with a product called **Beacon** (November 2007 to September 2009), launched on the overreaching premise that "Once every hundred years media changes . . . ," that posted selected activity elsewhere on the Internet back to Facebook. The product was initially only an opt-out function—meaning you had to proactively turn the feature off—causing a privacy furor over fears that information both harmless (that surprise birthday gift purchase) and not so harmless (that DVD of questionable content) would be broadcast to your five hundred closest friends. Zuckerberg had to apologize for the product and shutter it in the face of a class-action lawsuit. It would, however, be the predecessor of the opt-in and more successful Connect product that allows you to log into other sites and apps on the Internet and share actions and content back to Facebook if you so chose.

The development of **Sponsored Stories** (January 2011 to April 2014) followed. A sophisticated product that allowed advertisers to amplify actions people had taken with a business on Facebook—such as Like, Check-in and Offer redemption—to that person's friends. While effective—the "social context" of seeing your friend engage with a business proved significant in the awareness and effectiveness of the advertising—the product was complex and unpredictable to use and triggered a class-action lawsuit that Facebook had to settle relating to the use of people's likenesses in these ads. A crucial simplification of Facebook's advertising products followed. Focused on ease of use, sophisticated targeting and effective content types, it led to the renaissance of its advertising business.

"Failures": Acquisitions

Although Instagram, WhatsApp and Oculus VR make the headlines, you cannot expect your acquisition engine to have a perfect record.

Facebook acquired physical gifting service **Karma** (May 2012 to August 2014) to power its Gifts feature—especially around birthdays—to much enthusiasm in the market, which saw an opportunity for Facebook to participate directly in commerce—more than a billion users means more than a billion birthdays a year—rather than just encouraging it through advertising. The service, however, was not able to consistently grow engagement. Even if it had, the possible future complexity of Facebook having to be increasingly responsible for physical warehousing and fulfillment was a difficult premise against best-in-class providers like Amazon. Instead, Facebook focused on enabling retailers' key asset (the logistics of consumer purchase) with its own key asset (knowledge of and access to those consumers).

To aid another one of its key constituencies, developers building Internet services and mobile apps, Facebook bought software-as-a-service provider **Parse** (April 2013 to January 2016) to provide easy-to-use infrastructure services that allowed developers to concentrate on building and growing their services. In a story mirroring that of Karma, it would be Amazon and their Amazon Web Services that proved more adept and popular at the task, and Facebook once again retreated to its unique and lucrative asset (the ability to drive installation and reengagement of the developers' apps through advertising).

Although the story has not been fully written, Facebook's acquisitions for advertising beyond Facebook, including targeting and ad-serving platform **Atlas** in 2013 and video ad supply-side platform **LiveRail** in 2014, have not fared well. A complete rewrite of the Atlas technology and huge competition from Google's pervasive DoubleClick competitor has made adoption of Atlas a much longer road than Facebook anticipated, causing Atlas to be relegated to a cross-Internet measurement tool rather than its larger ambitions. Issues with the quality of LiveRail's content supply (sites beyond Facebook's own often suffer from click fraud by so-called bots not actually representing a human user and ads that are served but never seen) have caused wide swaths of the service to be shuttered to prevent degrading Facebook's own effective and high-quality inventory. Its homegrown Facebook Audience Network, an easy-to-use extension of ad formats and sophisticated targeting based on Facebook's knowledge of people to carefully qualified mobile apps has proven a much greater success on this front.

"Failures": Mobile Apps

Nothing is more important in today's Internet than the ability to successfully build and grow mobile apps. Facebook, Instagram, Messenger and WhatsApp are the premiere examples of the species and are all under Zuckerberg's control. That doesn't mean Facebook hasn't had its significant share of struggles on this front. Its aborted efforts number in the double digits.

Perhaps most famous among these is **Home** (since April 2013), a replacement of the Google Android home screen featuring a full-screen browsing experience of Facebook content and stand-alone messaging. As close as Facebook ever got to building its own mobile operating system or phone, Home managed to show that there is actually such a thing as too much Facebook, with most users who elected to download and install the functionality being overwhelmed by Facebook's seemingly taking over their phones. Technologies from the effort, however, made their way into more successful efforts, including Messenger and Instant Articles.

In its long competition with Snapchat for person-to-person and small-group sharing that appeals to Millennials, Facebook offered up

Poke (December 2012 to May 2014), **Slingshot** (June 2014 to December 2015) and **Riff** (April 2015 to December 2015), all meeting with little success. Offering simple messaging, ephemeral messaging requiring return messages and collaborative video editing, respectively, none of the apps showed game-changing differentiation from either Facebook's own offerings or those from formidable competitor Snapchat.

Launching to plaudits from across the industry for its engaging full-screen design, the reimagined (and curated) Facebook reading experience of **Paper** (since January 2014) also found little large-scale traction among users. Its technology, however, lives on in the new reading experience of Instant Articles (and the related advertising product Canvas) in Facebook's own mobile News Feed.

Similarly, **Rooms** (October 2014 to December 2015), pseudonymous chat forums for mobile, meant to address people's interest in connecting *without* authentic identity during the rise of apps including Whisper, Secret, Ello and Yik Yak, failed to stand out.

The **Facebook Creative Lab** (January 2014 to December 2015) launched to enable experiments like Paper, Slingshot, Rooms and Riff, was soon shuttered due to its lack of success and a distinct sense that creating an isolated team tasked with creative breakthroughs was not nearly as effective as spreading the opportunity—and responsibility—for these breakthroughs across all teams at Facebook.

The distributed approach, however, is also not a guaranteed success engine and can lead to puzzling stand-alone offerings like **Camera** (since May 2012), stabilized time-lapse recorder **Hyperlapse** (since August 2014) and collaging tool **Layout** (since March 2015) emerging from various fronts, including—and occasionally seeming to compete with—the Instagram team.

The Future of "Failure"

Along with all the failure has come enough success to feed a cycle of increasing scale of risk, more than occasional new failure and larger successes for Facebook. It's no longer just small coding projects. Instead, it's ever larger acquisitions, consumer hardware, and expansive fail-faster factories like the Connectivity Lab and the latest organized risk-taking effort launched in 2016, dubbed Building 8. Reporting to CTO Mike Schroepfer and headed by no less an organized failure celebrity than former head of both the U.S. government's Defense Advanced Research Project Agency (DARPA, which originated the Internet) and Google's Advanced Technology and Projects (ATAP) group Regina Dugan, Zuckerberg intends to invest hundreds of millions of dollars over the next few years on the team's efforts to build software and hardware systems beyond the mainstream of Facebook efforts. A full-fledged incubator with a separate COO, head of creative and business and technology staff, its seriousness cannot be questioned. After all, it was Dugan who labeled her group at Google—working on projects like 3D indoor mapping systems, modular mobile phones and 3D animation—a "small band of pirates trying to do epic sh*t."

While this upward cycle is the exact opposite of the toilet bowl of stagnation that occurs when some large companies constrict in the face of risk or fail to recognize that the worldview shaped by their prior success is being eclipsed by new forces, it does not last forever. Even Alphabet (Google's parent company)—who still needs to be considered the trailblazer when it comes to the heady mix of risk and failure now commonly referred to simply as moonshots in Silicon Valley—has had to curtail, focus and rationalize its speculative activities, including self-driving cars, healthcare devices, high-altitude balloons for Internet delivery in developing countries, wind farms and the reconceptualization of entire city infrastructures. And *they* enjoy as their launch pad the second-best profit machine in the world behind Apple.

Flying ever closer to the sun means some questions that Zuckerberg could shove to the back of his mind in the past now crawl into the light. How much risk is too much risk? Is there enough success among all the risk? When does trying to out-innovate Snapchat and not succeeding time and again become alarming and not just the natural order of competition (with *The Wall Street Journal* having projected in October 2016 an IPO for Snapchat parent Snap Inc. in 2017 possibly valuing the company at $25 billion or more this threat has never been more real)? What happens to all this upward momentum if the advertising business that funds all of it begins to show cracks?

When, in other words, does all that harder and faster "Failure" become just . . . failure?

The two Facebook "failures" closest to actually being failures in the sense of diminishing Facebook's current and future trajectory are its lack of progress in presenting a next-generation search experience across their own data as well as that on the open Internet and its apparent inability to grow successful new mobile products internally.

In search, Facebook has the two assets most necessary to do well: a search box at the top of its user experience and a leading slice of the time and attention of a billion users a day (search algorithms themselves are relatively commoditized at this point). Its display advertising business is a perfect adjacency to a search advertising business in competition with Google. It will need this asset as the opposite sides of the digital advertising chessboard we covered back in Chapter 8 will eventually grow to overlap, and maintaining revenue growth will have to come at least partially from taking share in digital rather than counting merely on money moving from television to digital and feeding Google and Facebook evenly. After more than five years of trying, however, Facebook is not appreciably closer to a unique and monetizable search offering that would cut into, much less displace Google's.

In mobile apps, Facebook's success beyond Facebook has come either from spin-offs of functionality in the main app (Messenger, Groups and Lite) or from acquisitions (Instagram and WhatsApp). Their original efforts have not been very . . . original, especially in their battle against Snapchat, the next most engaging mobile app and fastest growing. Their inability to put forth a differentiated, engaging product has forced Zuckerberg to play defense via acquisition. He has done this well with Instagram and WhatsApp, but it will leave Facebook exposed when the next acquisition refuses to sell or gets snapped up by Google instead.

Zuckerberg remains undaunted in the face of these issues. On the heels of announcing a breakout quarterly earnings performance in April 2016—at a time when stalwarts Apple and Alphabet had failed to meet Wall Street expectations—he made his intentions clear: "When I look out at the future, I see more bold moves ahead of us than behind us." (Admittedly, this rhetorical flourish also served as enticing context for the introduction of a new class of Facebook stock meant to keep Zuckerberg firmly in control of the company as he divests his command position to fund his and his wife's philanthropic effort, the Chan Zuckerberg Initiative.)

After a dozen years of successfully pursuing his mission, Zuckerberg—not unlike fellow large-scale risk-takers Larry Page, Jeff Bezos and Elon Musk—has given missions back their good name. To the extent that he "competes," he does so only with his mission and the time he has to execute it.

In that context, almost any risk is worth taking.

18

Nothing Lasts Forever?

No technology company is immune to disruption

Although Facebook has clearly outlasted its doubters, including screenwriter Aaron Sorkin, Google's Vint Cerf and Berkshire Hathaway's Warren Buffett and Charlie Munger, Zuckerberg knows far better than most that the list of *once* great technology companies is long and illustrious. Companies that in their heyday were not only leaders in their category but influential over wide swaths of the entire technology ecosystem for significant periods of time. Companies like HP, Yahoo, Intel, Cisco, Nokia and Blackberry.

Failure can occur swiftly via disruption—as it did in smartphones where Google Android and Apple iOS went from less than 20% market share at the beginning of 2010 to more than 80% just *three* years later.[1]

Or, perhaps worse, failure can occur insidiously in the guise of slowdowns that push you to the edge of crucial, trend-reversing action, but never over.

Death, Taxes and the Eventual Decline of Technology Leaders

Even the very best can come to struggle. Apple's year-on-year iPhone growth dropped to nearly zero in Q1 2016. Google contends with the curse of large market segment share in the slowing business of generating search clicks. And Amazon wages a constant battle with Wall Street to avoid expectations of profits even as revenues grow beyond $100 billion annually.

To have retained category leadership for a decade or more—as those three have—is a rare feat and a relative newcomer like Facebook is not immune to the forces that conspire to make that kind of long-term success so unusual.

Hope is not a strategy, so what's your best plan to resist those forces? Attack yourself before some*one*—or some*thing*—else does.

In the 1980s and 1990s, Intel taught the master class on this principle when it jumped from the commoditized computer memory market into the relatively nascent microprocessor market and showed the world the power of self-cannibalization by building ever faster processors. It's also how Apple went from a niche—occasionally near-death—computer company to the world's most valuable enterprise by delivering a *better* computer we could carry in our pocket and removing the word "computer" from its own name. Netflix was so serious about attacking its own DVD rental model—which had disrupted Blockbuster to extinction— that they put a streaming video-on-demand service in their name from the very beginning. And Tesla's $35,000 Model 3 is sure to cannibalize sales of its more expensive Model S, but if you're looking to change the very nature of global transportation, that's a small price to pay.

Playing Good Chess

Facebook—and Zuckerberg as its benevolently autocratic leader—have been very good at internalizing and acting on this most precious of Silicon Valley tenets by both protecting and expanding their neighborhood on the chessboard.

Has mobile become a big deal? Make the most engaging, most widely used mobile app in the world even as that reduces your traffic on the desktop website that was your origin. Maybe Facebook itself isn't the only answer in social media sharing? Great, acquire and grow Instagram into the *second* most popular social media property. What if social media won't be the biggest way people connect and share? No problem, spin out Messenger as an independent app and acquire WhatsApp, and grow each to a billion monthly active users. Is there a chance over the longer term that the mobile screen won't be our last screen? Maybe, so let's acquire Oculus VR and add a branch of VR and AR knowledge and consumer products to our business. Will new, more efficient models of extending Internet connectivity be necessary to connect the next few billion people? Most likely, so better have a Connectivity Lab that's not afraid to consider satellites and unmanned aerial vehicles in solving the challenge. Are computers finally powerful enough to learn how to be intelligent in more tasks than before? Almost definitely, so make AI—both researched and applied—a key across your products.

Facebook has smartly shared what are *not* core assets (software, server, network and telecommunications infrastructure designs) in order to gain industry-wide acceleration in the performance and cost reduction of these technologies and closely held onto the assets that *are* core (information about people and their connections).

And they have done it all before they *had* to. Former Intel CEO Andy Grove would famously say that "you never make the hard decisions too early." Zuckerberg has largely done an excellent job of facing difficult questions relatively early.

So far so good, but there is a reason that there is no place like Silicon Valley in the world—and the world has tried and tried: no matter how far to the proverbial west a young technology "man" has gone, in Silicon Valley there's always another "man" willing to strike out farther and faster. And sometimes you don't realize it until they're too far west to catch.

That's how, over the last 50 years, Silicon Valley has gone from semiconductors led by Fairchild, PCs featuring Intel, websites led by Yahoo and social services dominated by Facebook itself to today's smartphones and mobile apps, the attention for which is also primarily held by Facebook's family of apps. Now we are on the cusp of an evolution to mobile messaging with its leadership up for grabs, and the only thing that's certain about the future is that there will be another evolution after that. Only a few—Google, Apple, Amazon, Facebook—have continued to thrive through even one of these transitions, much less several.

Transitions in tech are like the Ides of March to Caesar: very dangerous to incumbents.

If it's so dangerous to be the leader, where does a dutiful follower of Andy Grove's "Only the Paranoid Survive" like Zuckerberg aim his paranoia, and what is he doing to prevent the long-term decline that awaits the vast majority of players in technology?

Threat Vectors: Internal

Facebook's success has put it in the privileged—but tenuous—position of every leader: controlling their own destiny through great strategy and execution. You don't just get a pound of strategy and execution from the supply closet, however, so **retaining great people** will be Facebook's biggest threat vector. It starts, obviously, with Zuckerberg who is irreplaceable strategically and culturally. Sandberg, Cox and Schroepfer are next on the list because they vigilantly run the most important functions at the company (business, product and engineering) and—perhaps even more importantly—are cultural touchstones for many thousands of others at the company, stirring the desire to hurdle the bars necessary to stay ahead. It's difficult to imagine replacing any of the people in this group, and consequences will follow if they were lost to the company—there is nothing accidental about Intel's struggles after Andy Grove ceded the CEO role or those of Apple following Steve Jobs' passing. The best Facebook can hope to do is to foster and build a next guard, and they are better equipped than most on this front. Facebook veterans like longtime Sandberg lieutenants Dan Rose and David Fischer on the business, Deb Liu on product, Jay Parikh in engineering, Gary Briggs and Caryn Marooney on marketing and communications and leaders that have recently arrived from outside the company, like David Marcus on product, have the rare combination of skills and culture fit to afford Facebook longevity.

A more insidious—and often harder to detect—internal concern for Facebook will be the **cost, breadth and distraction of speculative future projects** including virtual and augmented reality hardware and content, global connectivity and artificial intelligence agents. Exciting and necessary as it is to explore new frontiers, it is notoriously difficult to detect the moment when some of these efforts become too damaging to profitability and focus. When your ability to say no has subtly eroded to the point you can no longer rein in the chaos. When you're starting to throw good money after bad, propping up an offering your passion for which irretrievably exceeds consumers' awareness or interest. A thriving advertising business gives Facebook and Zuckerberg the means and intellectual air cover for these explorations, but over time this becomes a game of chicken between the growth of the core business and signs of sparks in the new fires Facebook is trying to stoke. Until Facebook has a second (search? messaging?)—or more diversified—business, Zuckerberg will continue to walk a gutsy tightrope. A similar challenge exists for Google, and we should expect to see the two increasingly invading each other's business to have better hedges for their respective positions.

Threat Vectors: Shifts in People's Attention

Outside the walls of Facebook, people's interests and behaviors will play the biggest roles in Facebook's fortunes. If **Facebook's leadership in broad sharing** between people is challenged by the continued rise of Snapchat Discover (more likely) or the resurgence of Twitter (less likely), Facebook's North Star Metric of engagement would clearly be threatened and, with it, its business. New features in Facebook's News Feed, including Live Video, 360-degree video and Instant Articles, and entirely new platforms like Instagram are meant to protect against this kind of insurgency and have done precisely that as the time people spend with Facebook offerings continues to rise.

A related but different challenge would be the **declining relevance of broad sharing** itself, as marked by the importance of person-to-person and small-group messaging including Snapchat in the United States, WeChat in China, Line in Japan and KakaoTalk in Korea. The growth of Messenger as an independent app and the acquisition of WhatsApp have put Facebook in the center of this shift and effectively protected their larger position. The bigger question will be whether Facebook lags in turning messaging into a profitable and growing effort useful for both people and businesses.

A third area to watch will be less *what* people are consuming and more *how* they are consuming it. A **shift in dominance away from mobile screens** would play away from Facebook's biggest strength and reshuffle the deck in ways not guaranteed to leave Facebook ahead. It is widely believed that to the extent anything will evolve (more likely) or replace (less likely) the mobile screen, it will be virtual—and more likely augmented—reality. That is why Zuckerberg struck with the Oculus VR acquisition many years before these new media are likely to have a significant effect on attention and consumption. Ironically, it was this acquisition that has significantly scaled the entire industry's attention to the technology, creating competition between consumer giants Facebook, Google, Microsoft, Sony and presumptively Apple to get to large-scale products—and the ability to redefine the landscape and protective moats—first.

Threat Vectors: Product Effectiveness and Revenue

In their current state, Facebook depends almost entirely on its mobile advertising product for its revenue. The reason the business is healthy and growing is that its advertising products are effective for businesses of all sizes all across the world, but a **decline in advertising effectiveness** would be a big threat to revenue and therefore to all dreams current or future that Facebook has in pursuit of its mission. That loss of effectiveness could come from issues in Facebook's own products (declining value as the amount of advertising grows or prices going up as inventory becomes constrained) and/or improvements in comparative digital advertising products including those from Google, YouTube and new entry Snapchat (fast becoming a top-tier player with eMarketer projecting nearly $1 billion in revenue for Snapchat in 2017). Facebook's highly diverse customer base of over 4 million advertisers of all sizes is a natural hedge against any systemic failure of the system, and a consistent stream of new offerings, including full-screen interactive Canvas ads based on Instant Article technology as well as so-called "shoppable" video and 360-degree video ads, is meant to deliver more value for more advertiser objectives.

More broadly, an **inability to grow—or, if necessary, acquire—the best new products** will stunt Facebook's pre-eminent position with consumers (by going deeper with its existing users in developed economies or being the provider of products to new Internet users in developing countries, which will count in the billions), the source of the industry's interest in its advertising business. The strength of its business and reputation as enabling acquisitions to succeed have put it in a good position to augment its offerings, but you're only as good as your last effort, and a failure to maintain the growth of its core business or to help an acquisition flourish will not only create a revenue hole for that generation but put the future acquisitions necessary to recover in question.

Threat Vectors: Host Platforms

A dependency that's easy to overlook in Facebook's tremendous success in mobile is that **it has two landlords** who are not entirely incented to make them successful. Apple's iPhone iOS and Google's Android are host to essentially all of Facebook's mobile engagement and therefore revenue. These systems are not "open" for any app developers to connect unfettered with consumers (the way the web works). Instead, they are gated by Apple's App Store and Google Play and by their respective terms and conditions, which are entirely at Apple's and Google's discretion. Of the two, Google is both the biggest competitor to Facebook as well as nearly 80% of the unit volume in mobile platforms, and the introduction of terms on the Android platform that are onerous to Facebook's functionality, especially around the nature of advertising, would be a direct hit to the heart of Facebook's business and revenue. While Facebook, Apple and Google exist in a triangle of mutual assured destruction—the phones need Facebook's apps, which are the biggest and most engaging, and Facebook needs both platforms—even a subtle disturbance of the operating conditions such as Apple or Google levying a tax on advertising in apps not using *their* native ad systems, would be bad news for Facebook.

Threat Vectors: Regulatory

Getting its wings clipped by government intervention seems like an abstract threat to Facebook until you take a closer look. Whether it is having its **availability** taken away outright (as in China) or intermittently (e.g., Vietnam) by communist governments or operating under **constraints** for reasons of data protection and privacy (e.g., European Union Data Protection Directive) or content filtering (e.g., German rules against the use of Nazi symbolism, certain Islamic countries' rules against the depiction of Muhammad)—any or all of these can make Facebook's pursuits more complex, limited or outright impossible. Particularly difficult would be regulations that significantly constrict the availability of data about people to improve Facebook's matching of advertisers to consumers or mandates—such as the rules governing media in the United States—that would throw off the News Feed algorithm's unfettered ability to maximize for user engagement. Facebook has taken great care to be actively involved with and responsive to the local regulatory conditions in all countries and knows that the only way forward is through genuine engagement and collaboration, a function housed in Sheryl Sandberg's organization and the subject of significant focus for Sandberg herself. The long game of partnership, politics—and, for Zuckerberg, even learning Mandarin—is Facebook's path forward in this complex minefield.

Imagining the Impossible

Taking a look at that competitive picture, Zuckerberg will have to continue to allow for the possibility that his current winners may be burning platforms. He must not only be cultivating the next platform to which he would jump if it came to that, but also diligently be seeking the *next* next platform in the distance. At Facebook's f8 Developers Conference in April 2016, he described this mentality as a three-step progression that (1) takes new technologies, (2) turns them into successful products with people and then (3) builds an ever growing ecosystem of partners like developers and advertisers around them. Facebook is an assembly line of different technologies at different points along this progression, with Facebook itself being the most mature ecosystem, Instagram, Messenger and WhatsApp being successful products maturing into ecosystems, and artificial intelligence, connectivity and VR/AR just beginning to evolve beyond the technologies stage.

To attack Facebook's technology assembly line, you would have to go after Facebook's key asset, which—as it is for all businesses—is the source of its revenue and therefore vulnerability.

For Google, their unique asset is understanding people's expressed intent, which translates into revenue via search advertising. For Apple, it is the superior integration of hardware and software, translating into highly profitable gadgets with vibrant software and content ecosystems as their revenue.

For Facebook, this asset is its leadership in connecting people and monopolizing their time spent online via the things that happen across those connections. They translate that extensive access to people into revenue via display advertising.

To make all these threats and maneuvering more real, let's imagine three very specific, very dangerous scenarios that could unseat Facebook (beyond the failure to execute the plans they already have, the most urgent thing to protect against for every leader):

Attacking head-on (next five years): There's nothing easy about going after Facebook's ability to connect people and deliver content across those connections, but the combination of a fast and popular newcomer and the financial, technical and awareness-generating wherewithal of an established leader could drive a wedge between Facebook and people just as the nature of sharing appears to be going through a transition to being less personal.

The most potent allegiance on this front would be Google acquiring Snapchat.

In a move not unlike Facebook's acquisition of Instagram, this would allow Snapchat to concentrate on growing their platform for sharing short clips of media in mobile settings beyond its strength among Millennials while taking advantage of Google's financial air cover, existing content generation ecosystem from YouTube—where more than 2,000 channels have over a million subscribers[2]—and giant base of search and display advertisers, the largest in all of digital.

If Google further combined this offensive threat with the unprecedented defensive move of changing the terms and conditions of its Android mobile platform to allow advertising in apps—including Facebook, Instagram, Messenger and WhatsApp—only if those apps (1) use the Google advertising system and (2) allow Google to take 30–70% of the resulting ad revenue, it would mark a simultaneous erosion in Facebook's strategic position with people *and* advertisers as it would syphon users away from Facebook's apps and cut revenue for as many as 80% of Facebook's users by more than 30%.

There are a number of unlikely elements in this scenario—not the least of which is the antitrust scrutiny Google would be under for forcing the Google-based advertising system on its app ecosystem—but, it is feasible.

Flanking (five-plus years): Instead of going after Facebook's strength in connecting people, the flanking approach would go after how people spend their time online. Currently, there are only three successful competitors to the amount of time Facebook's family of apps corner: YouTube, television from the likes of ABC, CBS, NBC, Fox and ESPN delivered via cable and satellite providers and subscription video on demand (SVOD) from the likes of Netflix, HBO and Amazon Prime Video.

This approach would leverage people's interest in video content of all types—and their growing inability to understand and digest all of it as it seems we now have too much television on television—to pull people to a new offering with which to spend their time that throws a highly intelligent, easy-to-use umbrella over all sources of video. To be viewed as a game-changer by people, the service would have to pool paid content from the key traditional and SVOD television players, as well as key public content from platforms including YouTube, Vine, Snapchat, Instagram and even Facebook and lay over that entire collection a next-generation discovery mechanism that goes beyond today's mechanisms, which can no longer adequately address all the content. Instead of search, guide or store approaches, it would offer an intelligent agent that actively surfaces the most interesting video for you given all available public commentary and trends and your continued reactions and guidance.

A butler for your content: a "jukebot."

It will have to do it all—from the NFL to HBO's *Game of Thrones* to Netflix's *House of Cards* to that trending Vine to the new Snapchat Discover content from CNN and the 360-degree video from the Red Bull drone races in Dubai—for $99 per month, delivered on-demand to all the devices you care about, saving you from higher cable bills and combining what today is spread across many different apps and several different pieces of hardware into one integrated and interesting experience that never runs out.

Although difficult to deliver—only Google, Apple and Amazon have the means and scale to pull this off—it would force Facebook into a battle royal to decide who the real king is: People or Content. Whether machines or people are the best way to get to the content you enjoy the most.

If that service can be launched at a time of large-scale transition to a new primary interface, such as consumer-grade, lightweight, wireless glasses capable of going from being completely clear to delivering both augmented and virtual reality—an 80-inch television anywhere you want it—and do so substantially ahead of Facebook's own Oculus VR hardware while also blocking Facebook's existing services from becoming as popular on the new interfaces as they have on mobile, a significant threat to Facebook's momentum would be created. Every minute you spend with a "jukebot" is a minute you are not spending with Facebook's News Feed, the major source of its revenue.

Both Apple and Google have seen how Facebook co-opted their phone platforms for its own momentum and success. An evolved content and interface future could provide the disruption and transition necessary to shake off Facebook's hegemony in a similar way that the smartphone eco-system shook off Intel's dominance during the PC era.

Revenue incursion (five to 10 years): Perhaps facing even longer odds than the first two scenarios, but no less dangerous, is the one that goes after neither Facebook's strength in connecting people nor the amount of time people spend with Facebook but instead simply goes after a part of its advertising revenue by providing a more effective advertising option for a fraction of Facebook's advertisers big enough to disrupt Zucker-berg's momentum and clip his ability to invest in the future to protect against disruption.

Aside from Google, online retail giant Amazon is one of the few com-panies in the world with a pool of knowledge about people as valuable as Facebook's. In important ways to advertisers, Amazon's knowledge might be even more valuable.

With purchase history—and credit card numbers that shrink the dis-tance between interest and transaction to a single click—for over 300 million people worldwide,[3] it's no wonder that the online retailer is al-ready a more valuable company on Wall Street than retail juggernaut Walmart. By 2016, Amazon's Prime membership program had pene-trated into 50% of all U.S. households and 70% of its wealthiest.[4] Early experiments with its Dash buttons enabled automatic reordering of household items with just the push of a button and its Echo voice-controlled assistant eliminated even the need to lift a finger in ordering. Beyond running its own online retail operation, Amazon had also ex-tended its ability to run the infrastructure of digital businesses to compa-nies small and large by growing its Amazon Web Services division into a $10 billion annual operation in less than 10 years.

With highly respected and longest-tenured[5] Internet CEO Jeff Bezos at the helm, who is to say Amazon could not become even more focused on turning its knowledge of people at its own site and those of companies whose infrastructure it manages into significantly expanding[6] advertising opportunities for companies that would otherwise have taken their money to Facebook, especially in the retail and consumer packaged goods categories that are consistently two of the top three largest spending categories in all of advertising?[7]

The sheer number of if's around these three scenarios show just how difficult it would be for even large competitors like Google, Apple and Amazon to unseat Facebook's lead with people and the way they spend their time.

It's not impossible, but it would be a long shot under the best of circumstances, and Zuckerberg has shown clearly that he will not stand idly by or be caught asleep at the switch.

Acknowledgments

My family—Lynn, Chris and Katrina—the greatest social network a guy could ask for, and the ones that give me *that* look when it comes to taking the next risk. Love you!

Facebook's advertising team—Mark, Sheryl, DRose, Murph, Jake, KX and all the great teams I had the very good fortune of building with—who let me come to the other side of the table.

Facebook's leadership headed by Mark and Sheryl—one of the greatest CEO/COO tandems ever—and Chris, Schrep, Jay, Chamath, Javier, Alex, Naomi, Fischer, Gary, Kevin, Mike, Jan, Brian, Lori, David, Yann, Brendan, Palmer, John, Michael and one of the deepest management benches in Silicon Valley—who have the vision and the will to build Facebook toward its achievable-unachievable mission.

My friends and the community of more than 1.7 billion people who fill all of it with life.

My agent Jeff Herman for envisioning this story to begin with and tirelessly taking up the cause of a first-timer. My editor Stephen S. Power for trusting me to put this on paper and giving me the fantastic guidance and amplification to dramatically improve it.

My friend and writer of great female lead characters Adam Rakunas who helped me place my foot during the first step of this long journey. The gracious friends who were willing to be early readers and commenters, including Robert Siegel, Dennis Carter, Ann Lewnes, Gokul Rajaram, Deborah Conrad, Brad Boston, Pete Clark, Geoffrey Moore, Annie Wilson, Roberta Thomson, Will Platt-Higgins, and Marc Pritchard.

Managing editor Miranda Pennington, senior development editor Barry Richardson and copyeditor Fred Dahl, typesetter and interior designer Sabrina Bowers, proofreader Julie Grady, and creative director Cathleen Ouderkirk for ensuring the quality of the finished book matches the quality of its subject, and director of publicity Irene Majuk for quarterbacking the effort to get the word out.

And AMACOM for giving the best untold story in Silicon Valley voice and reach.

With all the gratitude only a rookie can feel.

Notes

Chapter 2

1 According to The Chronicle of Philanthropy, Zuckerberg and Chan's 2013 gift of 18 million shares of Facebook stock—worth $1 billion at the time and over $2 billion by 2016—to the Silicon Valley Community Foundation (which focuses on economic security, education and immigration integration) was the largest charitable gift on record that year and the largest ever by a donor under 30. They had donated another 18 million shares of Facebook stock to the Silicon Valley Community Foundation the prior year as well and have also given to other causes, including $100 million to the Newark New Jersey school district, $75 million to San Francisco General Hospital (where Chan works) and $25 million to fight Ebola as that epidemic raged in the African continent in 2014.

Chapter 4

1 Facebook-commissioned studies, 2014 and 2015.
2 *The Information*, February 2015.

Chapter 5

1 Facebook data 2005–2016.
2 Facebook data 2009–2016.
3 Alexa/SimilarWeb, January 2016.
4 Internet and population statistics in this section courtesy Internet World Stats, November 2015.
5 Ericsson Global Forecast, November 2014.
6 Ericsson Mobility Report, June 2016.

Chapter 6

1 Nielsen Brand Effect, May 2012.
2 Salesforce Ads Benchmark, July 2015.
3 eMarketer (citing Social Brand, Firebrand Group and Simply Measured), April 2016.

Chapter 8

1 Google and Facebook annual reports, January 2011.
2 Google, Q4 2010 earnings report; Facebook S1, February 2012.
3 ZenithOptimedia, December 2011.

4 Statistic Brain, June 2015.

5 Facebook, Q4 2010 earnings report.

6 Google, Q2/Q3/Q4 2011 earnings reports; comScore, July 2011.

7 comScore, November 2010 (193 million); Google Q4 2011 earnings report (350 million); Google announcement June 2012 (1 billion).

8 eMarketer, September 2015; McKinsey & Company Global Media Report, October 2015; Magna Global, December 2015.

9 Activate, Inc., October 2016.

Chapter 10

1 Arab Social Media Report by Dubai School of Government, May 2011.

2 Statista, January 2016.

3 Strategy Analytics, January 2016.

4 Internet Society of China, "Public Pledge on Self-Regulation and Professional Ethics for China Internet Industry," http://www.isc.org.cn/english/Specails/Self-regulation/listinfo-15321.html.

5 *The Economist*, April 2013.

6 Chinese state media sources as reported by BBC, October 2013.

7 Tech in Asia, March 2016.

8 Statista, January 2016.

9 Statista, January 2016.

10 Statista, January 2016.

11 Strategy Analytics, March 2015.

Chapter 11

1 *Harvard Business Review*, December 2015.

2 *Allstate–National Journal* Heartland poll, 2014.

Chapter 12

1 Google and Facebook S-1 and quarterly earnings reports.

2 August 2012 *Fortune* magazine article on the ouster.

3 eMarketer, October 2015.

4 comScore, September 2015.

5 comScore, December 2015.

6 Facebook, April 2016.

7 comScore MediaMetrix US, December 2015.

Chapter 13

1 Facebook, Q4 2015 earnings report; Twitter, Q4 2015 earnings report; WhatsApp company announcement, February 2016; Tencent, November 2015 earnings report; Rakuten, June 2015 earnings report; Line, December 2015 earnings report; Statista, July 2016; *estimate using Snapchat May 2015 company announcement and 65% DAU/MAU assumption; **estimate using Kik August 2015 company announcement and 65% MAU/Registered assumption.
2 Enders Analysis, 2012.

Chapter 14

1 All data in this section from internet.org State of Connectivity 2015, internetworldstats.com, November 2015.
2 A 10% increase in broadband penetration has been shown to lead to a 1.35% increase in GDP.
3 Cellular Telephone Industries Association (CTIA), January 2016.

Chapter 16

1 United Nations, June 2013.
2 eMarketer, April 2016 (projecting Internet population of 4.2 billion people by 2020).
3 Charles C. Mann, *1493: Uncovering the New World Columbus Created*, Alfred A. Knopf, 2011.
4 Alfred W. Crosby, *The Columbian Exchange: Biological and Cultural Consequences of 1492*, Greenwood Press, 1972; and Alfred W. Crosby, *Ecological Imperialism: The Biological Expansion of Europe, 900–1900*, Cambridge University Press, 1986.

Chapter 18

1 Statista, February 2016.
2 vidstatsx.com, April 2016.
3 Statista, Jan 2016.
4 Piper Jaffray, April 2016.
5 Bezos founded Amazon in 1994.
6 According to eMarketer 2015, Amazon was projected to make $1 billion in advertising in 2016.
7 Kantar Media US, June 2015.

Index